Mouths, Tigers' Mouths

Sophia West

Published in 2003 by Onlywomen Press, Limited, London, UK.

With financial support from Arts Council England

ISBN 0-906500-76-1

British Library Cataloguing-in-Publication Data.
A Catalogue record for this book is available from the British Library.

Cover design: SPARKdesign

Typeset by Cynthia Fayers, Cardigan, Wales.
Printed and bound in Great Britain by J. W. Arrowsmith Ltd., Bristol.

Contents

Introduction

This volume is, simultaneously, a celebration – as a flowering of poetic talent always is – and a lament for a life, and a gift, cut off too soon.

Sophia – my daughter – was born in 1962, and died in 1996, of suffocation during an epileptic seizure. Her malady – about which one poem survives – was the result of a sledding accident when she was a small child: harsh, early instruction in human fragility, whose mortal implications she could never entirely disregard. Perhaps because of the scar that ran down the centre of her nose, she was always leery of conventional ideas of feminine charm, viewing these as a politically weighted ball and chain. Instead of preening for oppressive males, Sophia demonstrated against the Vietnam war at the Seneca military base, in upstate New York, got thrown into jail, marched in the Gay Pride parade, and wrote poetry.

She was, from her earliest days, stubborn and brilliant, with an acquisitiveness bordering on voracity toward attractive accidents of information, language, style. (I remember an incident when she was three or four: a sudden, repetitive chant, shouted louder and louder, of a name that caught her fancy: "Macchu Picchu, Macchu Picchu. MAACHUU PIICHUU!"). Her reaction to sounds that pleased or amused her – to odd combinations of words, arresting repetitions, curious shades of meaning – suggested a bright-eyed raptor, always on the alert for a nourishing morsel or pleasing bauble to seize for its treasury. For Sophia as a poet this meant dreamsongs – for example – a pantoum, "nos morituri" (all appearing in this collection). These she stored in a "magpie's nest" of a mind (her father's description of his own mind) to await consideration – or deployment – at her pleasure.

Sophia West was born in New York City in 1962, of mixed British and American parentage. Her father, Anthony West (himself a writer, and the only child of the British writers HG Wells, and Rebecca West) was living in New York at the time, a regular contributor to the "New Yorker" magazine. Her mother, Olivia Emmet (that is myself) a translator of French and Russian texts, belonged to a large clan descended from Thomas Addis Emmet who arrived in America following the failed Irish Rising of 1803. That event – including a Speech from The Dock by Thomas' younger brother, Robert, condemned and executed by the British – became a paradigmatic symbol of Romantic Irish nationalism. In my youth, the Irish writer, Frank O'Connor told me that Robert Emmet was as responsible as anyone for the advent of Romanticism in ireland. At the turn of the XIXth and XXth centuries, the American Emmets were known to their kinsmen, Henry and William James, as "the Emmetry".

Sophia's early childhood was divided between New York during school terms, and an old farmhouse in the woods, behind Stonington, Ct. In 1972, when she was ten, the family moved to London, where Anthony West was researching and writing his biography of his father, HG Wells. Although the move was in many ways a difficult uprooting for Sophia and her younger brother, Adam – the loss of familiar faces, places, assumptions – the upset also proved fruitful, providing, as it did, a set of alternative lenses through which to view the world. Instead of the East River and Central Park, there was Primrose Hill, with its prehistoric hill fort, looking south, over central London, and school in Harley Street, with a Headmistress, whose demeanor seemed echoed by her name: Mrs. Fiers (whose pronunciation was close to the word "fierce"). This coincidence very much pleased Sophia, always ready to be amused by serendipity. Moreover, in the case of Mrs Fiers, a stern manner veiled a warm heart. On stressful public occasions – like the viva voce conjugation of latin verbs – that severe countenance tended to soften as Mrs Fiers urged on a faltering young charge: "Come along now, Old Sausage: no need to make such heavy weather of it: Amo, Amare, Amavi, Amatus!".

As well as the sensuous particularities of living in England – the landscape, architecture, voices, weather – Sophia enjoyed acquiring an acquaintance with some of the people and places of her father's youth.

Although she never met Wells – who died in 1948 – Sophia enjoyed her encounter with her grandmother, the brilliant Dame Rebecca. Despite the famously difficult on-again-off-again love-hate relationship between Rebecca and her only child Anthony, Sophia and her grandmother were on cordial – even affectionate – terms. In the early 1980s, when Sophia was studying for her A-level exams, in London, she met Rebecca comparatively frequently, for lunch or a cup of tea. Curiously (reflecting, perhaps, Rebecca's complicated attitude to men) Sophia and her half-sister, Caroline, were the only direct descendants mentioned in Rebecca's Will. Each grand-daughter received a small legacy; but of male descendants (and there were three of these) the Will made no mention.

After her years in London, Sophia – who did not take kindly to regimented study – passed through a year and a half at the Putney School, a "progressive" boarding school in Vermont, followed by Hampshire College, in Amherst, Mass. Recognized at both these establishments as a gifted student and promising writer, Sophia (to the chagrin of various pedagogues, and the considerable anxiety of her parents) steadily refused to adapt to school conventions and expectations. Eschewing organized education, she chose, instead, to live at a variety of feminist collectives – in Seneca, New York, and ultimately, in Oakland, California, across the water of San Francisco Bay from the city of San Francisco itself. An intellectually acquisitive autodidact, she was widely read in literature both ancient and modern – in the European classics, as well as writers of the present day, both European and American, and authors from modern and medieval Japan. The poems that follow contain quotations from – or references to – works by authors as diverse as Francois Villon, Virgil, John Berryman, and WB Yeats, as well as experiment with an exotic verse-form, the Malay *pantoum*.

Several of the poems in this collection have Lesbian texts – or subtexts – with a sense of camaraderie and safety when the subject is feminine, and an alarmed ambiguity toward the presumptions of maleness and masculinity, which are often perceived as dangerous.

Whatever the subject, however, these pieces evidence particular and promising poetic gifts: an ear alert to properties of language, to shades of meaning inherent in words, and sequences of words, and to the sonic effects produced by repetitions of consonants, vowels, and syllabic sequences. The text is also lit by two perceptions that might, at first blush, seem contradictory: a relishing of physical beauty, as a basic constituent of life, and – equally fundamental to Sophia's world-view – a sense of irony.

The poem "guilt, clouds, plums" provides an example of this particular poetic alertness. In each of the poem's five stanzas, guilt, rigidity, nothing, expression, exclusion, are expressly mentioned, occurring and re-occurring, functioning as key words, both in a sonic sense, and as meaning. As the poem proceeds, these words – with their painful and cumulatively punitive burden, or "pin-prick", are combined – or contrasted – with the idea of fluidity, of "fluent turmoil", a condition in which "there is nothing rigid".

There is "…nothing rigid//in the wind – nothing rigid in still air...nothing//come to that's really rigid in the world (exclude//perfection...)"

Mean and rigid forms (to which, the poet says, she is drawn by guilt) exclude natural expression, and nourish nothing: there is nothing rigid in the world (except perfection), and even then – if conditions of perfection are attained, there's always the inherent possibility of failure: failure to sustain, retain, maintain. That guilt, of course, is fluid, like almost everything else in this world, and "adaptable to any circumstance". Rigidity imprisons, creates imprisoning masks that leave nothing of one's vital center exposed, or visible, all pain and fear drawn "deep into some center that excludes// me even…"

As the poet slowly picks the mask's lock, "exclud(ing) //old voices that insist on the expression//of inflexible principle" she stands "…for truth…a rigid// martyr, perfect in suffering…"

The poem's final stanzas proffer a vivid alternative to imprisoning rigidity:

"sunwarmed plums//waves of satisfaction", and a recognition that "…there's nothing//I crave more than this". "No rigid abstractions in this fruit…!"///

Many of these poems are infused by a declarative, even declamatory sexuality that is strongly Lesbian, thrown down like a gage in the opening poem, and continued, as a running theme, throughout the collection. Sophia chose to believe that "The Patriarchy", and its inherent asumptions of male supremacy, must be challenged.

The first poem, "Remembering the Hard Lesson", introduces the idea that maleness means peril: the city where the poet lives is described as "gray with garbage sad with// cheap decay//rotten with men... dangerous". "Perfection", introduced in stanza 4, is reductive and confining, "...closing//out profusions of curves and warmth//shutting out confusion refusing/ to admit a rose// or me if I open and open if I// speak if I am a woman am a// vine or a serpent a figleaf//blown off my mouth or//mouth...". "Perfection is afraid of my mouth my// womb my crooked teeth..."; is afraid, that is to say, of bloody, ungoverned femininity. Sophia was a passionately sympathetic reader of Robert Graves, a believer in the Muse, in the White Goddess, in female challengers to the pretensions of Appolonian classicism. The city is a "homicidal lie" that "crushes/our lives against a silence unless//we speak...". But if "we" (that is, women) *do* speak, then "suddenly our mouths are roses"; "suddenly our mouths are tigers'//mouths..."

The speech of roses, of tigers' mouths – a natural feminine capacity, as Sophia saw it – is, above all, what she wished to celebrate.

Olivia Emmet

From Journal #80

Remembering the hard lesson

Remembering the hard lesson, bitter
silence that wraps me in itself
tighter and tighter   the more
I look away

These days I live in a city
gray with garbage sad with
cheap decay rotten with men
a hard place dangerous challenging

sometimes blessed with wild
tufts of fennel fluffing through
pavement   bright vines and roses
confined but glowing
little moons and suns reminding

me voices live in nature   the
constant eruption of blooms and
buds   leaves the dark tears of trees
wept into this city's scab   a scar
taut on the earth

remember perfection confines itself
to itself smaller and smaller closing
out profusions of curves and warmth
shutting out confusion   refusing
to admit a rose

or me if I open and open   if I
speak   if I a woman am a
vine   or a serpent   a figleaf
suddenly blown off of my mouth or
mouth

remember perfection reduces itself always
to identify with nothing else   spreads
a steady rash of sameness
perfection is afraid of my mouth my
womb my crooked teeth

this city a homicidal lie
dislikes our single purposes crushes
our lives against a silence unless
we speak
suddenly our mouths are roses

ii.
suddenly our mouths are tigers'
mouths

our voices live in nature

remembering perfection without fear

the following poem is dated 6/14/90. A later, typewritten revision was found, and is presented here.

guilt, clouds, plums

I have always been drawn
by guilt
to mean and rigid
forms- they exclude
natural expression,
nourish nothing.

Clouds pass writhing above me; nothing
interrupts their fluent turmoil. Drawn
slowly across the sky (her expression's
always changing), across the gilt
sun's pinprick, they exclude
no shape or motion- there's nothing rigid

in the wind- nothing rigid
in still air, either- nothing,
come to that's really rigid in the world (exclude
perfection, and the painful way we're drawn
to it- and even then the guilt
of failure's fluid- adaptable to any circumstance for it's expression).

I look in the mirror for ages sometimes- my expression
is unreadable to me. It took a while to learn that rigid
stare, unlearn emotions. Guilt
made a mask that hid me from confusion and left nothing
on the surface- pain and fear drawn
deep into some center that excludes

me, even. I slowly pick the mask's lock, and exclude
old voices that insist on the expression
of inflexible principle above all else, insist the lines are drawn:
I stand for truth (whatever hurts the most), a rigid
martyr, perfect in suffering, fearing nothing
but self-indulgence- strangled in ecstasies of guilt.

I'm eating sunwarmed plums just off the tree; guilt
between hand and mouth interrupts briefly,   but can't exclude
waves of passionate satisfaction. Really there's nothing
I crave more than this: each deep expression
of recognized pleasure. No rigid
abstractions in this fruit that's bursting under my teeth! I'm drawn

to live without an ounce of guilt. Expressing
this is new to me but I exclude rigid
insistence of any kind: the nothing on my face is overdrawn.

Another Go At It

The cats are playing on the floor
wrapped around each other, wrestling.
In the night-lit kitchen
crying and making sudden jumps

This morning in bed we lie naked together
Wrapped around each other, wrestling.
We investigate each other, laughing
In the warm dusk, the shades drawn.

Wrapped around each other wrestling,
skin against skin, singing together,
in the warm dusk, the shades drawn
I think of our long-time loving, happy.

Skin against skin, singing together,
It's natural to be here, safe
I think of our long-time loving, happy
we're lying here so trustingly.

It's natural to be here, safe-
I know you now, I begin to believe
we're lying here so trustingly.
Face to face we lie smiling

I know you now. I begin to believe
all the hard times, bitter times, good times
Face to face we lie smiling,
touching each other gently

The hard times, bitter times, good times
wrapped together and wrestling
touching each other gently
ahead of us and behind us

Wrapped together and wrestling
we've strained against silence, struggling-
ahead of us and behind us
the fears we refused to face

We've strained against silence, struggling
to love to tell the truth
Fears we've refused to face
Change as we look in to it

To love, to tell the truth
Simple things but it
Changes as we look into it.
Succumbing to love is not
A simple thing but it
Gives me your strong eyes
Succumbing to love isn't
Beyond me I finally know.

Gives me your strong eyes
Looking deep into me and
Beyond me. I finally know, it,
Back and forth, moving together.

Looking deep into me and
Not choosing any distraction
Back and forth moving together
We're face to face and smiling

Not choosing any distraction
The cats are playing on the floor
We're face to face and smiling
In the night-lit kitchen.

My First Pantoum *by Luna age 27 April 8th, 1990*

Sometimes I wonder about my mind
I have been reared to doubt
the things that happen to me,
to question what I do

I have been reared to doubt
Myself, I am so ready
to question what I do
without faith in the future.

Myself I am so ready
to surrender when I could hope
Without faith in the future
Fear of failure is hard to dismiss

To surrender when I could hope
Even though I am so stubborn-
Fear of failure is hard to dismiss
When everything seems uncertain

Even though I am so stubborn
I sometimes get worn out
When everything seems uncertain-
Small moments of joy must sustain me

I sometimes get worn out
Trying to remember everything and understand it-
Small moments of joy must sustain me
The things I've seen and felt.

Trying to remember everything and understand it-
A task too large for my busy mind.
The things I've seen and felt
Are drops of water easing a parched land

A task too large for my busy mind-
I wonder why I feel I must strive for it.
Are drops of water easing a parched land
Enough when I could hope for rivers?

I wonder why I feel I must strive for it.
The absolute stillness of fact might not be
Enough when I could hope for rivers-
Free flowing passions moving me wildly.

The absolute stillness of fact might not be
All that I really want. When I dream of
Free flowing passions moving me wildly
It's true that I'm afraid but I could risk it-
All that I really want when I dream of
Freedom is knowing the truth and power of my feelings-

It's true that I'm afraid, but I could risk it-
Courage could take me into satisfaction.

Freedom is knowing the truth and power of my feelings.

Something I've wanted since I first could think
Courage could take me into satisfaction
Beyond the layer of fear I've been forced under.

Something I've wanted since I first could think
Is space to recover from my own mistakes
Beyond the layer of fear I've been forced under.

To find the joy of learning without shame
Is space to recover from my own mistakes-
I yearn for innocence for trust and love
To find the joy of learning without shame
And centering in myself I'll find the power.

I yearn for innocence for trust and love
Sometimes I wonder about my mind
And centering in myself I'll find the power
To question what I do.

From Sophia's folder entitled "First Versions"

I'm tired of being kept wound up like this

I'm tired of being kept wound up like this
I'm tired of being told it's not my business
The American way, the American way

I don't want to make it the American way-
that's back to back
or face to face
baby you are violating
my personal space
the American way, the American way

you got your good
you got your bad
your American tradition and your
Superman

you got your apple pie
it's an absolute
like your fourth of july
and your man on the moon
the American way, yes it's the American way

you are deified
in a factory
average is the way to be
aim high for mediocrity
the American way, the American way

you'd like to think that you're all the same
your hygiene and your plastics and your rhinestone frame
you charge like a buffalo to normality
but you can't avoid diversity
we don't all get to go to university, though it's
the American way, the American way

you hallucinate, it isn't opportunity
blame the faggots and the niggers and the kids today
this isn't the way it used to be
in the gold old days
we had the American way

but you got to go with the flow
you got to run with the stream
it's not consistent baby
but it TASTES NICE
if you don't look too hard
the American way, the American way.

dated 29 April '83

Africa on Television

Imagined Africa- o living stone: harsh
hot and unready sand
sharp darts: the fleet paws, prey-
leap beast; and where
killed eland's hot tongue dries.

hunter behind pale rock,
spear in a single
eye-flick flashed to the
fast-felled
flesh of a swift
meal; death, and unwatered air.

hard soles cracked
leather limbs, oil, and
drawn moisture; ritual; from
desert tubers.
Shining tribal, National Geographic nudity

(love like hot-heated
desert haze dry bodies rolling in
parched grass: tawny)

imagine, africa. Wide place-
lion
leapt and tore sand.
hero:
a painted man,
rippling glazed, brave: dizzy.
Immense; the sky
time seems less frequent here. It seems.

In Which the Lizard raises it's Squamous Head

Just me and my elegant shadow-
She's all I need, I seek solution in
her dark flat double silhouette
running beside me.
Love is death, though not
the popular Elizabethan annihilation by orgasm,
not the little death- love is surrender.

Certainly Love's no fat
winged boy-child, impish and random,
his aimless arrow
singing in saddened breasts-

Nor the dark-boned dancer of doom-laden
etchings, seductive skeleton
snatching virginity with rattling hands
from hapless maidens;

My shadow's an elegant woman:
she's well defined against the pavement's
grain- condescending, she
chooses to follow me, whether I ask or no.

Love is a gray slick lizard;
Oozing from marshy ponds
It scours, devours-
Greed is its name, a demon
only hunger summons.

In Which the Lizard raises it's Squamous Head *(revised)*

Just me and my elegant shadow-
She's all I need, I seek solution in
her dark flat double silhouette,
running beside me-
Love is death, though not
the popular Elizabethan little death- love is surrender.

Certainly Love's no fat random boy-child,
or aimless arrow
singing in saddened breasts.

No dark-boned dancer, doom-laden
snatching with rattling hands
virginity
from hapless maidens.

My shadow's an elegant woman.
She's well defined against
the pavement's grain and
condescending, she chooses to follow me,
whether I ask or no.

Love is a gray slick lizard;
Oozing from marshy ponds,
It scours, devours-
Greed is its name: a demon
only hunger summons.

Pome

I.

Being drunk on a sofa
in front of the tube

II.

What's this business of an
appropriate tone?
Some sort of
storyteller's rhythm, a
hypnotic roll of a phrase
to draw the
suckers in?

Form over content- Jesus Christ
WHAT A DILEMMA
(I mean what do you go for?)

Over the weekend down in
the city on Tenth and A
Sliding around a
dingy basketball playground
drinking beer out of a paper bag
and bullshitting with four
friends in a monotone...
they go to the SVA and
make displays with
klieg lights

Me on the other hand now
I talk a lot and
drink a fair amount of beer
on a small blank island
in the middle of a
rainy winter

JESUS CHRIST

And going for the
normal conversational and

deadpan tone
because it fits a disgusted
frame of mind

(Here's where I say something
piquant about the decay and
the seedy commercialist
unresponsive flatulent
continuousness of
fast food franchises and
Ordinary People, just like
the pungent movie)

Or do I go for ART and
HONESTY and
RISK and swing my
Tarzan ass out over the
plumbless void of
SELF RESPECT, and is that a
personal or a political decision?

III.

What's real life and
what's imagination?
O deep, Sophia. Very deep-
Mais ou sont les flippin neiges
d'antan?

I. Elizabeth

Thin white grimacing
baby girl in
glasses, short brown hair
she fidgets on a red maroon leatherette bench on the ferry.
the stretchband waist of her
flowered yellow corduroy trousers
doesn't cover up her stretched pale belly
under the tight blue t-shirt.

II. Elizabeth's Mother

Elizabeth's mother is
fat and 20
in cheap drab clothes
she heaped on her seat
smoking,
her hair is
blonde long dry and
matted in fat curls.
Pale blue eyes huge behind her glasses
glazed.   She sucks her teeth and sighs.

III.

These people it seems to me are like rocks
worn down   worn down, and sealed tight, and separate
all they expect is to go on being
where they are and how they are
they bother each other
"Why does that other person want to burden me when
I'm already dead with
troubles of my own?   my life's so
heavy, heavy   I can hardly
raise my eyes without dying.   No matter what they tell you
it's all the same.   No point exerting yourself,
won't get you nothing, never did, it's all the same."

A silver body dusk dappled dream-tossed surged half-waking and rolled over, with semi-somnolent heaviness threw an arm across its neighbour.

"Oh love, oh love love love," sang a shrill bird in the dreamer's ear. A bird like a factory whistle trying to talk fire-engine. "Love love," said the feverbird and flying off, Clara Santaclara opened her eyes heavily and sighed. She was not comfortable. The bed was too narrow for them both. She and Alma lay like silver statues in attitudes of stoic discomfort; Alma slept on, frowning. Clara dug her chin into her elbow and stretched with a heave. The bed complained noisily and shook and Alma opened a questioning eye. Clara waved dismissive and Alma groaned back to aching sleep, the vicious cradle of Morpheus' arms.

Slowly and carefully Clara rolled onto her back feeling the sand, bread-crumbs and miscellaneous grit that strewed the sheets digging sharply into her buttocks and sleep-red thighs. Her skin was pocked by the grit and rubbed raw by the woolen blanket now binding her ankles painfully. Raising herself on her elbows, she surveyed the room.

"Oh my God what a mess," she remarked to herself, closing her eyes. The room was filthy: books, blankets, catfood, broken pens, moldy silverware, beer cans, bits of cigarette, fly blown fruit and almost everything else that Clara or Alma had seen that summer lay in heaps, spread in fields, clustered in drifts of dust and mouse shit. "Oh God God God," Clara repeated inwardly and reached without looking for the alarm clock on the bedside table. Several walnut shells were knocked to the floor as she groped for it. It was 8.00 AM and, as usual, much too early. Alma would sleep for another two hours possibly. Clara lay back, her spine pressed against a leaking ball-point pen she had forgotten in the bed last night. As she rolled her head in anguish on the pillow, the pillowcase hissed against the pages of an open notebook bound in heavy green paper. The corner of the notebook tickled a pimple on the back of Clara's neck. She stared at the ceiling, unable to move without disturbing Alma, who was now breathing as though dreaming of drowning.

"Oh God God God oh God," she whispered through lips caked with dried and peeling skin, "Oh God." Not that she anticipated assistance. The morning weighed like lead on her aching eyes.

"Pain is the correlative of insight," she informed Alma in a calculatedly inaudible voice. "The Lord created the heavens and the earth."

Alma groaned and threw an arm across Clara's face so that her lower lip was pressed sharply into her teeth, twisted by Alma's elbow.

Some white disgusting muse

Some white disgusting muse
feeds on my heart
O! lily, oh green spine-leafed acanthus spite
that maggot harridan-
Feculant sprite-

I had thought
to remember you in a
solemn poem

What words would I have
like a clear clarifying and illuminated mist
spread 'round your features

your face like the slicing knife
beautiful of Time
unchaste of fantasy

I had thought
to remember you in a solemn poem

clean white branch of a
spreading moonbare tree in
sharp winter

ice frosted clarity your
eye like a shining on
a frozen river brown with the
deadened rush of leaves

at midnight how perfect your
neck like the laughing
arm of some mythically all-powerful
soldier in a glorious victory

riotous warmth of green
colour-rioting summer:
heat-washing love-

how many beaches have we picked shells along in
druggèd fantasy of
sharp exact sight?

my love my love
I remember you in a
poor verse

how sweet your lips
unbent and wet
your mouth conceals me forever
in dark warm forests

so bodies are
like colliding stars
ungathered in loose-fitting words

your hands with whip-tight wrists
long lily-fingered hands

Laugh I will laugh with you
because you believe in the possibility of
Rightness
You think a thing can be shaped
by its completion
How sweet is your confiding faith
wrapt in your vase-like belly and
your swaying dancer's back
how you trust Time

Here I will trust you forever and
envy your shadow
As your faith carries you to it's
proof with unnecessary flaunting of it's
benediction

Here I will desire you;
I am unpeaceful
my soul is a darkening
Here I will desire you:
white illumined light surrounds you.

Love is a dangerous subject-
Why write about some
pink thing and its
pulsing, deep in the fog fuzz of
popular imagination?

Flowers bowers roses poses kisses blisses
heroes and dainty misses
sighs and eyes and cold replies
tragic magic melancholy,
youthful folly- a cloud of saccharine attributes
obscuring one's vision, swarming and
making it seen

one hopes to get what one will not
Why write about love?

For an Iranian woman in chador on a 'bus in Kensington.

Hello, black
sack – your nose
shellacked, your eyes
are flat, your
body's wrapped- deep, dark, in that flowing black-

elegant she is but
nonetheless docile, and
asexual, and submissive, a
little bovine; 50 rigidly maintained paces
behind her man; the 'bus had to wait for her-

her hands when seen
are flashes, blurred-
rapid light claws- her
glance is hard.

nevertheless she sits on a
'bus in Kensington while
the conductor a Jamaican
drunkenly sings some slurred loose
song, sexy as all get out, and I
stare at all of her that shows
while my Dunhill burns down in my hand

your eyes they say are amber jewels
I'm so curious I'm so confused
lady why do you do it? With that dark bag
hiding your mouth
who knows how you smile?

[*alternate last line:* I'll never know if you smiled.]

saving my energy

saving my energy
for some
future freedom, I'm always
battered down and beaten down
tight hatched. Don't I know, what They will say or do. Have done.

things I might say if
I thought I had an opportunity
but awareness of the consequences of action
is dangerous

It's politically required of me
to be active and
hopeful. But awareness of the consequences of action
is dangerous.

why should i make metaphor?
It's euphemism.
Meanwhile out there, there is, as they say,
the world

One woman in a
cheap restaurant-   I watched her
eating fried eggs for lunch
and yelling at her child.

"See mama, I got a fork. Just like you."
"Don't spill that on you!   Shut up.   Put that down."

she hated the baby because
she couldn't afford it
shining little energetic three year old
bouncing and smiling
doubtfully but hopefully
she doesn't understand why her mother doesn't want her
but soon she'll know – money, just money.

They're not going to even think
about trying to change it. Soon the daughter will hate the mother too.
Awareness of the consequences of action
is dangerous.

From Journal 82, Sophia's last journal, which opens dated Jan. 7, 1996, with the last entry dated Nov. 25th. The following poem is one she transcibed from an earlier notebook.

The Anthem of Womanly Purity

A sign of splendid failure is
More worthy than a mild success
A bitter sucking at the fruit
Of Glory and Achievements missed

The ideology of loss
Is built from this familiar cross
Abstention is a noble thing
When no one – absolutely no one – is as good
As mighty, as we could have been

With prim delight we smile upon the pain
And festering, festering weals
And pussy sores
That holding all our Genius in
Has sewn across our tender skins
Over the years
"FOR SILENCE IS THE SPIRIT'S FIELD,'
Fainting we sigh from narrow Virtue Love

Reviving only on this sour suck:
The Things We Could Have Done, With Luck-
Distilled into a thin pale soup
On which a hedonist would choke

Turning our hearts from comfort, hope and peace
Our Banner is: No Glory in Release!
The rocky path of our most noble way
Is but for those evolved, refined, spiritual
Yet humble as ourselves, we softly say

Whose selflessness is Boundless and Complete
Has climbed the Sacred Mountains of Defeat;
Therefore she's Mighty who without a face
Lives on this Earth and dies, leaving no trace.

dated early April, 1996

bitter after head-void shakes

bitter after head-void shakes drool from a moment away,
girl under heave and pound of
rusty thinking
moans-
then need like iron
incubates life:
blood aches above smooth time.

That, in case it is not clear, is about a seizure.

what lakes want and say and ask
will urge like gorgeous sweat:
"over here- essential beneath skin- licking sky,
cool lust for blue has you.
use my still beauty
take my water tongue,   my sun-hot easy music
chanting a lazy beat, a flood shot from some spring storm-
bare your fast juices in me-
I am - I am - I shine -
go on - use me -
please, friend-
swim."

Song: To An Aggressive Analyst

I like to leave a barbed clue to
follow me, in little light-
the dusk of shadows, jungle-green-
a footfall, heavy in the leaves.

a bird disturbed in radiant flight
could shriek a hint: the whereabouts of one who dropped
soft as a raindrop
out of sight-

slipped between branches high above
the writhing floor where in the grass
harsh apes baboons and smaller beasts
chitter distressed/ at sudden sun/
stabs them at parting of wide vines.

I like to leave a faint but clear
mark at the place I disappear/
evaporate like parched-out dew:
a ghost of humidity
in the light
that blinds rude hunters in the groves.

From "First Versions"

ME AND MY FRIEND ON NATIONAL TELEVISION

I.

1. Do you know I love you
bit her full of love
                                        SHIT: IT'S SHIT: SO WHAT: SHIT?
that what we- it's fecal!
soft brown ooze must mean you're
relatively healthy; relatively: relatively healthy-

pomes penyeach.   LITERARY VERY
out of most pence reach.   LITERARY: LOVE-

2. Yes. I love you   WHIPPER, SNAPPER
bit, her full-of-love: bitter,
full of love, like
burst fruit, maybe: MARCH PAIN

eat you! my carnivore my   SPLIT LIP IT WAS
mid day   meal

3. We love you all   JAW
what sweet fat lip   GENTLE
huge exopthalmic I   GENTLE
meet.   JAW
your lip I sweeten it that   HOT
spit-wet tooth on   FOOD-
lip-lost tongue   KISS

4. The Immediacy of the Experience

o i was in it in it lip I was in lip in lip:
wet lip wet lip in, in it I was lip I was lips in lip-
                                        LIPSTICK MURDER MIRROR A
biter, full   of   LOVE GAME   biter bit
                                        SHE SAID
love bit   her   IF I CAN LOVE YOU   love bit h
full of   BODY HATE ME BITE   full of
red raw. . .   love
                                        (sleep-flesh sweet sleep and breath:
bright
                                        it might it might be it might be

II.

it was dream and I wonder why
I was in it. If I had done it
out of a dream what would it have
been. They would have made it.

it was dream: I bit her, full
of love. No doubt. Her wet flesh.
Drooling. But never waking would have
done it. Waking it would have been real.

What might a love have been. I
haven't seen her for years in a
month. There were the others. She would
have screamed. What she said. I did.

What might it have meant, this.
I dreamt. That blurred film. And
bitter, full of love, I bit her. Blood
was a bland bright squeeze.

A magazine. She's not like that, not
glossy. Where did we get it? And
hurt my- hammered my head with- ache-
she's not like that, not like an ache

I wonder why I was in it. It was
a dream. I saw her. What we did.
A dark. A fly couldn't hurt her.
They made it, said to me. Bit her, bit her.

You have to treat him like he's famous

You have to treat him like he's famous
because in his head he's famous
and in his mind-
well, there's just about everything.

I met a boy called Geneva Unconventional
he's a little crazy, a trifle *odd...*
he wears a yellow leather waistcoat and
reads his poetry aloud at hardcore concerts
(mostly benefits for worthy causes-
US OUT OF EI SALVADOR was the last one)

I never heard him read, but
I have a feeling he mostly shouts.
Hardly anyone goes to those concerts-
The last one I was at said
be here at nine
it didn't get started til one a.m.

but Geneva's famous; his friends say so

Even when frowning (he hates crowds)
he turns from 13th St. to Avenue A
all skinny leather shoulders and
hunched up skulking stride. He says he's famous.

The only thing I really know about him
is- once in the trendy Park Inn he sneered
at my fat wallet- thought all the old bus tickets
I forget to throw away were 20 dollar bills-
"How they do it," he said "I don't understand".
But I was drunk, I was trying to talk to him about Art,
because Geneva's famous.

Staring Match for Mythic Cowboys

the brother poker: buzzard-bare the other joker: grimed greasers and locos
stud-hats glares of fat rot, whispers of curses which
shitsour and fewer when ready beware
stripped-silver gun;   great fate impress the mother poker in motions and
life or fear-hard neck and resistance

uphill faint plots in sight: tote
dead Cain in slippery
slow sweat   the slick dead hero

(harmonicas: who made them-
thick tin spit   a toot a trump a knockdown blowing horn
them lizard boots so
sharp of toe   your outward chest and
inward trunk   and
final box   she was his sister so she
said before that burst...
                                        it was a shooting pain and now
your gallons all are drunk your horse is
pie your girl
is gone your boots   are damn well hilled
and Mom-   will never know-   )

G + H in Jungle *(First Version)*

the color ochre: mustard-glare
mud-flats
sweet sour and sewer where
streaked palette knife
or brush it a
dark vein in
fever marsh of
waste
jungle a pulse in
vein   and sharp shivers

the color ochre: blind
stare of fat hot
heavy
sun   - great weight oppress
hard neck and
faint in sight float dots
down slippery
sweat that
big explorer

painters and doctors and
sisters of mercy who
prepare

the color ochre

in oceans and distance.

Gauguin and Hemingway in the Jungle

the color ochre: mustard-glare the color ochre: blind painters and doctors
mud-flats stare of fat hot sisters of mercy who
sweet sour and sewer where heavy prepare
streaked-palette sun great weight oppress the color ochre in oceans and
knife or hair-hard neck and distance
brush faint dots in sight float
dark vein in slippery
down sweat that big explorer

When once we rise

When once we rise
Late in the afternoon
The fat skies
Bloat with a fever swoon
Your Thighs,
Pressed unpleasant red
against the wrinkled sheets
of sleep-tossed bed,
and cramped feet
Lie like the heaviest earth
Along my side
And my
Ripped open eyes unwide
So unserene
Are cruelly molested
by the scene-

Our aching arms
Stale from excessive rest
And over-warm
Big veined hot breasts
Unwillingly since our wakening

How Horrid
The remnants of our torrid
loveswoon
We have lain
Androgynous shepherdess
Androgynous sated swain
Till afternoon
How bloodless flabby is our flesh
Lord how I love you
Lying in bed too late-
how sick-
Professors of an unclean fate-
So we kiss
And then
Forget
As you are
Bliss-

Out one night in Greenwich Village

Out one night in Greenwich Village
after the café hours had slid
into the darker hours of
artists' bars, to drink

with a crowd of shouting and
drunk friends, whose
hair was black, whose hair was red,
who shaved their heads or
had 1000 braids and wore

black biker jackets and velvet
dresses and pink leather
mini skirts and
vampire lipstick and chattered and
yelled and smiled-

I saw through the silk grey haze of dawn and
the disinterest of beer
an old white birdhouse, jammed

haphazard into a tree in the park,
just past the iron railing; it
had a glow off the moonlight,
perched in the fork of a branch,
as though it were the house

not of a bird but a very small peasant
who had been blown
by a humorous hurricane
into a tree, in the dark green
light grey wet flat rustling park.

Rhoda had a Panda

And the funny thing is, the funny thing is, is it didn't hurt a bit, said Carolus, twinkling at the barn door with a trilapsed gillieflower in appurtenance. Slowly the madaque made helmsmen of the laud, knowing the belly was inticate and passing over. Strange though it may well come dancing across a seldom corrected manifest, Lullipet went more to seminary than actually velcro. Though murder, she sanded a pelican. Her demipuppet gallopped down Demarest and pushed a christening to the flowershow. Maude got faded. The windowmost concession trillopped sloppily back.

unfinished transcription

Zelda

She's very thin in
a photograph angular as
some natural medieval saint
with her pelvis tilted
forward flat hard
and bony,
she might
be allegorically a captain on
her bridge outstaring
her wallowing sea
but the hang of
her bright white skirt
and the uplift in her lifted
eyes, her vague
hand clasping mild hair
to her stony skull
absently as in a
breeze, her shins stark
hard and bony as bird's legs shiny
and wellwaxed make
her a ghost of an unwifely
wife; the dark real
secret of the Gibson
girl: *it may not be*
and *it cannot endure* mixed
equally with *it must*

whether finally she was
more resigned than
desperate is hard to know.
They all had parties and
were very brave, they
had manners in
savageness of wit and
grace- very
up in the air their
sex and their dancing had
little gravity it
spun, silver

and glass and tin and
gold like chandeliers
and fountains, very fast
and free, drunk
for awhile with
flight they flew
like jazz and
glamour. What to
do when things
began to slow?
To be discarded if
you slow too soon.

Rhythmless Dreamsong for Bell, Drum and Jester

In green you
stand so
visionary seen and churchly chaste: a
marble monument to
some abstracted, woman-virtue
In a grove you
stand naked so
strange wandering line a dream
what is it what is it?
The air dances
'round you like a
veil or a mystery
so your hidden self
shines
you are a golden coin
unreal
so expurgated version There in that dream-grove
straight upstanding goddess statue
armless and immensely
dishonest monument
To poetry

so like a Botticelli
There Aphrodite perhaps with your
modest hand
dappled in leaflight
you silent and unmoving
stand
your hair is like a waving net of
finest strands
so like your purest robe
the setting sun
bathes your most pallid
flesh
you are
white as a mad and merciful
unviolent nun
fanatically passive/There
caught/in a web of trees

soon
dark erases you and flamingly
vanished
you will still hold a glow in your
taintless/absence-

echoically fractured circumstance
we
who beneath glass wave of
fortune dance deprived
of promise, or authority-
oh do not ask, what is it...

echoically fractured circumstance:
that insubstancèd second of the
carnivorous clock
one
wild violent tick of ceremonial magisterial
most ivory imperial
religious clock

echoically fractured:
that sight unseen, that
dictate of the first blind instant
WE WHO ARE ABOUT TO
love
shall fade away and fade away and
sin no more

Oh love!
Echoically fractured circumstance,
The light darts golden in the jaded sea

Bodies awash
away
The sighing swain
crack'd on the conscience
by sweet
Apotheosis-of-the -instant
What we love
What we love

Is always and forever
distant...

Echoically fractured circumstance
what time we seize
certain of no reprieve
gone
we are gone
and wasted in the moment
love.

Claims Made By One Who Is Falling From A Cliff.

Lord, have I prayed in pagan fields
and screamed in sheds-
begged transience of bricks lodged
solidly in complacent sun-bright walls,
Have I dreamt
White fields of faces falling through
Hissing air,
have I
bless daisies for each sweet dead
drifting falling petal.
I have become
Walls and dark wooden rooms where
oaken chairs stare tensely at the
sundappled floor
I have often given winter white trees the
sparse furthest blackest tips of their
straining branches
An eye is my imagination it
breaks shards of the least perceived days
to dust of their fat shadows
Their ripe black fecund shadows
My unwinking eye
Catches the edge of dark as it
swims around blind white moons
I have
Fallen to my feet in the centre of
endless fields I am
calling long leaves from the middle of
summer trees
My song edges darting through
blinking rivers- Have I
stolen each night from its end and
piled it on
futures of sweet frost stiff star corroded wandering?
Then I will
pull black dirt-veined boulders bodily from
recalcitrant earth and
Lift the sky that dangerously hooks itself on
times like these-

Fragment

Ode
to a Geode:
O thou
compacted node, lode-
stone stowed so
deep beneath the field
congealed crusted thick concealed, an
unrevealed monster midget-
rock in dark
pits, far abysses; abcess rock,
you canker stone
chipped, knocked and carved by
'sauri bones and
scored by heaps of
magma, smooth irregular sphere-
O Grendel turd! you
calcinated petrified egg of
stony bird,
tacitum ugly lump-

Far from me

Far from me
Is my love and
she is

Far though I should
Turn in my white bed hoping
Her there

She is
Not near me and
Though I long for her

Though I
Sing slow songs of her
Quietly

Wishing her by,
She is
Far from me

And I will not see her soon.
Though I call after her
I am like a bell
Ringing resolutely against silence

She is far from me and
Though my hand aches from
Not touching her smooth-ribbed side
I am like an eye
Longing for absent light.

Little song for a pygmy woman

I.

Breasts like sandbags swinging as she walks
her hut with branches
and wide leaves, sweat
shining in
her hard back's rhythm.

II.

She says the forest's her
mother and lover: when it
dies, then she will too.
The only thing she wears
is a loincloth of pounded bark
dyed red with red wood
and fastened with vines.

III.

she smokes tobacco in a
huge pipe with her sisters
and watches a man
writhing in a rope of leaves.
He's playing a hunted elephant
quivering under the precise spears
of the tiny hunters.

When they break camp she
floats into the forest and
is invisible, silent-
a small dark leaf
circumspect and expert
loving her mother.

Soft day indeed

Soft day indeed it
was that bore her, hot,
in some
far Hawaiian mist, or before that,
in an orphanage
before her parents
bought her, though I
know nothing of her, and
she knows nothing of her,
before then- those days
she hardened her feet on
steaming rocks running
past bursting fruit without
question-
daughter of an Army man,
taught
close to the steaming waves and
white sand to be unquestioningly an
American

that later I might
meet her in cold
harsh snow dazzling and
steep hilled, ice-ridden and
frozen streets of
Montreal, pale city-

that later we might
follow cach othcr in aeroplanes
across grey oceans
green stormy below us

that down Dublin's
streets rainy spattered
herded with
poor men mad women their
begging their childrcn
we might, soft day,
walk together

frightening prim
spinsters
who duck at us their
bright mouths
tight pursed
with our intimacy
our smiling our
loose limbed ease and
hope

that later we might be woven softly
together bright,
radiant, in the silver
night, laughing
softly together at the
harsh wind blustering,
the owl's hard
screeches in
the moon's wide eye: it's stony light-
soft day that bore her.

From loose papers found separately

sometimes I think

sometimes I think
I think too much
sometimes I
wonder if I know enough

no I know I don't

well I am a woman
that is the first thing
I suspect

and all that means

a womon a womon

first is that something to mourn?
Well no
we all know
that is not so-
no woe
in womon.

but then I am bright shining and
enthusiastic as
a crisp
apple
and it is not so simple
not just one single
thing

a womon a womon

and all that means

and I despair and
do not desire to despair but
nevertheless I do, though
I aspire to

do more
I do aspire to
more than that
as who should not

and then I wonder

what to do
what to do
I wonder
what to do

the first thing
is
one thing to
hold onto
a clutch to grip
a crutch

and of course
the first thing
is
an axe
bitterness

a labyris and
the sum
of memories
dismembered
and remembered

womon a womon

and myself
after all
after all
after all this
the first thing
is
myself

a womon a womon

Some days I want to

Some days I want to
hold out my heart
red and heavy in my
tidy white clean hand
trim as a flower,
hold it out to you
bright
like my desire
across the ocean
which is silence.

Pull it out of me, maybe, through my
chest on a bloodtight vine
and raise it
like a beating lantern
a beam
across the sea to
move me
faintly into your mind
as a dim dull echo
of days we spend differently
in different towns
in different weather
working our ways through time

(an abstemious red bird
preoccupied by many
similar songs
will fly
distractedly from my blood;
a red erratic
butterfly will
dip and swing over
the seamless sea and
whisper
in your ear).

Other days
I press it down deeper into
my belly, nurse it
like a stone dedicated to sorrow
carved with hard, sour lines
and knotted figures,
symbols of impossible obstructions

deep down in my stomach
it beats out
a thunder drum, hard to support
and shakes me, ruins me
with love.
I'll push it up in my mouth
if I can and taste
the thickness of the salty veins
lyrical on my tongue, I'll shout my
heart across the ocean-

Most days my heart sleeps solid
under it's usual flesh, thuds out
discretion and necessity,
declares no longing, dreams
of recognition. O love, I murmur
in expectant sleep, turn in my bed, reach out,
discover solitude

The following work is from Journal #15

It's hard to be discreet

It's hard to be discreet
In the middle of the street
Actually
We take ourselves so seriously
(at least I do)
And people say, you know
I'm strange
or deranged
Because...
(well I don't know why
but I think it's something like
this- you just don't sit
In the middle of the street
and write)

I wonder what would happen
I mean its hard to say what
exactly
If I think too hard, especially
But to be (just for a moment) serious
It does make me quite nervous
Afraid really
of being called (AGAIN) loony

tell me clearly . . .

tell me clearly goddess let it flow through me
what it ought to be what is the right way
for me
tell me clearly goddess I am not sure how to do
what I need to do how to move through this time
what I need to find
Or even let me know what I want to know so
much already but still I don't know how to know
what I want
Don't know what I want except that I want
really to feel a passionate want for something
some way
I need to be on my path I have the will but
where is the way   I know   I am on my path
but where is it going
Give back to me goddess my passion my flame my
snakes my symbols make me a priestess again
a true follower
of the sources of power let me remember again
the moon the grapes the dark branches of sleeping
trees Goddess remind me
my foot on the earth in one path my hands
working energy to webs of light
Give me again my desire to be healer to step the
circle and reweave the web to feel again the
nature of nature in my nature
the music of its power the power of its music
Goddess give me again my power
give me again your power again the power again

A white turtle

A white turtle ate a fastmoving young man for breakfast and reached within for a sense of majesty. The long beach bloomed into despondent afternoon.

"Why oh why are there no mellow fungi?" sobbed the turtle, pacing a slow and steady back and forth between two leaning palms. The sun smote flat against the fishy waves and stuck in white blocks across the choppy sea.

A song rose unprovident from the wet lung of the drowned boy, a burble of phlegm and bubbling sea flowers. Ants in red armor pinched across a flabby arm.

The turtle stopped and chewed thoughtfully on the bloody digits. Crack of wet bone slid against her slow jaw.

Diri, the Queen's sister

Diri, the Queen's sister, lifted the porcelain bowl to her lips again and drank, savoring the rich and subtle smell of winter tea, admiring the red horses who galloped forever against the deep brown background of the bowl. She smiled at Hekia and touched her lover's long, bare, muscular thigh. Sleeping Hekia groaned and shifted on their bed, goosebumps riding on her shin. Diri rose from her squat by the fire and quickly spread a blanket across the sleeping form. She drained the bowl of tea, taking a moment to chew the spicy dregs, then in two steps crossed the floor of the circular toti and swept past the quilted curtain that served for a door.

"Let no one disturb her, Meripa," she told the young womon who sat, wrapped in warm blankets decorated with Diri's house sign of red horses, by the toti's entrance keeping witness for the spirits that travelled with them this winter. A wild scent of burning herbs rose from the brazier at Meripa's feet and its familiarity made Diri smile. She gave the shelter sign to her niece and touched her quickly on the cheek. "The queen is at home?"

"She has not yet left her toti, Aunt," Meripa said.

"When Hekia wakes, tell her I'm with my sister the queen," Diri moved off even as she spoke and Meripa smiled to see the strength of this womon who strode proudly across the frosty ground, clad only in her inner shift, at an age when many women would not feel ashamed to huddle all winter at the storecity with the babies and the grain.

Tukmaye, startled from her sleep, jumped up still shaking the dream from her head and made the ward sign automatically, before she saw who it was that had come.

Diri laughed and pulled gently at the old priestess' wild white curls that stood like white fire around her wrinkled face.

"Tukma', sweet one, the herbs have lulled into sleep," she scolded, smiling. "Have the spirits left my sister's toti?"

Tukmaye snorted dismissively and without a word held open the curtain for her friend. Diri hid her smile and ducked into the dim interior. The central fire had burned down to glimmering coals and Yarmar, her emaciated frame almost hidden in her robe of blood red leather, stood swaying among the embers. Her eyes were rolled back into her head and a thin almost inaudible high pitched whine escaped her lips.

"Tukma'!" Diri whispered as she came to a startled halt one step into the toti. "What does Yarmar have to do with my sister?"

"Ssh," came back Tukmaye's muffled reply from outside. "The queen has called her."

"Leather in the queen's toti," Meripa affirmed with wide eyes. "Diri saw it herself or I wouldn't tell you." She absently swept a dark lock from her face and pushed another log onto the small fire she shared with her cousins out by Diri's picket line. It was close to the dawn, the dark was beginning to thin and the stars to fade. The breath of the horses rose in warm gusts onto the freezing air. For warmth, the young womyn had pushed their makeshift nests of blankets between the horses and slept two together, but even so the cold made it hard to sleep and they passed their time in tales and gossip.

"But Yarmar?" asked Huis incredulously.

"Yes, *that* old thief," Meripa assured the three sisters. She took a long drink of winter tea from the flask that they were passing back and forth, and continued. "Tukmaye herself was *asleep* by the entryway- what do you make of that?"

"Oh, bad magic," Uhinna said gravely. "Meripa, I am afraid- what does this mean, Yarmar singing in the toti of the queen?"

"But what did Diri *do*?" asked Ahiro, the youngest sister, as if she expected Diri to have challenged Yarmar then and there.

"Nothing yet, Ahi," Meripa sighed, and took another drink. Ahiro began to cry, and pulled the blankets over her head.

"Tomorrow she'll tell you what she meant by it," Hekia said hopefully but without conviction. She sat on the edge of the sleeping platform and watched Diri pace back and forth across the dark toti, scarcely visible among the shadows cast by the thick quilts that hung from the toti's curved walls and ceiling. A single moonbeam threw a narrow band of light from the tent's central smokehole and briefly lit Diri's scowling face as she walked through it.

"Yarmar." was all Diri could find to say, the bitterness in her face beyond measure as she thought again of Demak. A memory she rarely allowed herself for the pain it caused. Hekia sighed, remembering too.

It seemed impossible that Dolmiri could have forgotten her and Diri's sister even after these many years, but a queen had reasons which other womyn did not always straightaway understand. Hekia tried to believe.

"In leather." Diri added, as if daring Hekia to contradict her. "Blood red. Does Dolmiri grow *afraid*? she hissed out the last word with a look of rage upon her face and Hekia turned away, unable to comfort. "The priestess Tukmaye *slept* by the doorway, Hekia-Tukma' does not sleep when she watches the door. *What does my sister do?*"

Sophia wrote this story on one of her many visits to my home. We would invariably drink tea and talk in the kitchen, or she would read on the sofa while I folded my laundry or did the dishes. Our relationship was never well defined but I got great pleasure and calm out of those weekly visits. Sometime in 1996 she asked for some paper and a pen. I gave her an old notebook and busily went about my tasks. It wasn't until the night before her death that I stumbled across this story, that I had forgotten about and never read, after trying to return her last phone call.

Once upon a time, there was a little boy who was very very sorry for herself. And she had good reason, believe you me! He lived all alone in a little rickety lean-to shack made of mildewed matchbooks on the Lonely Planet Made of Papier Maché.

Now, as you know, this is a very little planet (one per customer); the crust is only one foot thick, and then after that it is entirely hollow all the way across (which is about 300 miles). In the very very middle of it, there is sometimes a certain secret something, which you might call volatile.

Now this little boy was not exactly a little boy, in fact she had lived on the Lonely Planet Made Entirely of Papier Maché for the last 5,000 years; but that was not judged to be relative or pertinent, in that (due no doubt to the planet's obdurate lack of rotation) time did not pass there- and so the little boy did not age: she only grew more and more bored, and at the same time, more and more frustrated. She was considered to be a very bad and ungrateful little boy, by the angels in charge of district 9 (which is where Gustavas'- that was her name- particular Lonely Little Paper Planet was to be found). This was held to be so, as she had been granted the gift of eternal youth, without having to sacrifice anything- so far as the angels could see- in return. But Gustavas was not happy. For the first 4,000 years she had run rampant around and around the crisp and easily penetrated planet, looking for things to do- and even inventing them, when they were not to her found. Once she invented a stampede of wild horses that she had to capture one by one. That was a particularly fine adventure, until all the horses had run out. But later on, it got more and more difficult to sustain her belief in these manufactured or fictional crises, and gradually little Gustavas gave way to a deep, apathetic depression. It was very sad to see her, sitting kicking her heels against the doorstep of her dilapitated shack, spending all her energy in a fierce pout.

Now at the same time that Gustavas was moping away on the Paper

Planet, a little girl called Maybelline was having a very difficult time on a planet all of her own. *She* was living on the Thumbtack Planet, and was very cross.

The Thumbtack Planet, of course, is a huge planet made out of enormous multicolored flat-headed enamel tacks all shoved into a big pink styrofoam ball. There are cracks and crevices everywhere, and it is very difficult not to trip up unless you walk very slowly or crawl. Maybelline lived in a house made of string woven around popsicle sticks, which was always tripping her up or twining around her head or limbs in inconvenient ways- catching on her spectacles or winding around the buttons on her flowered pinafore. She was much too busy being irritated to be lonely.

Now Gustavas had been on the Paper Planet for 5,000 years, but it seemed to him that not a single day had passed, but rather the opposite case was true for Maybelline- *she* had only been on the Tack Planet for 2 years, but it whizzed around so quickly on its axis, and she was so constantly concerned with trying not to trip and fall, or with unwinding bits of string from herself, that it *seemed* to her that 5,000 years must have gone by. She could not remember anything in her life but string, tacks, curses and the very annoying noise of wind whistling in between the points of the tacks where they stuck into the styrofoam ball.

Needless to say, neither Gustavas nor Maybelline was very happy. But neither of them would have been in a position to do anything about it- if not for a *strange coincidence*, from which we learn that it is genuinely a good thing to grab an opportunity when we can. For who knows if we will ever have the chance again?

Well, what was this strange coincidence?

It came to pass that one of the angels in charge of district 9 began to feel a certain dissatisfaction with his work. He began, that is to say, to Examine his Conscience.

This is highly unusual, for an angel. Once you have been described, even by your job title, as inherently perfect, the need to challenge this description generally falls away, and smugness, like tooth decay, begins its slow and evil work.

However *this* angel (Yvette) was startled out of smugness by the sting of a mosquito which woke him from a nap, and during that single instant of startlement, he began to wonder if everything he was doing was entirely correct.

Could this be heaven, Yvette asked himself, when so many people were plainly discontent?

It was very puzzling to him. In deep distress, he abandoned his post and went away to consider the balance of power in the Universe.

Yvette, as it happened, had been the Area Supervising Angel in charge of Local Planetary Rotations (district 9). That is to say, he made sure that all planets kept the same distance from one another at all times.

When Yvette abandoned his position, *all that changed.* Over the course of time, Gustavas' planet and Maybelline's planet swung closer and closer together; eventually Maybelline, staring stubbornly outward in a fit of pique, met Gustavas' dull stare. For the first time the two children had met another person.

"OO the 'ell are you?" shrieked Maybelline furiously.

"OW the fuck should I know," Gustavas muttered, chewing her lip.

"Your stupid match shack is going to get all tangled in my string thing, matey", Maybelline bellowed.

"Wot if it does?", Gustavas replied, but by now his attention was somewhat engaged- and her vegetative mind began to operate more and more energetically. "I tell you wot tho, love, it these two bits of crud fell into each other they might turn into something halfway decent."

"Alright," Maybelline smiled, "'Eres looking' at you."

And suddenly the two microplanets merged in cataclysmic chaos. What happened after that you must imagine for yourself.

Sophia and Cassandra White were both incarcerated for their protest against the Seneca, NY military complex. Their crime was that, together with a large group of women, they had dug a hole with spoons and slipped under the fence to peacefully demonstrate, by trespassing, against the existence of the nuclear-equipped military facility. Sophia wrote the short story in August of 1984 while they were both in the Metropolitan Correctional Center, which I believe is located in New York City. She wrote the story for Cassandra.

A small story without an end

Once upon a time in the middle of a forest in a large and sunlit clearing all covered with soft brown pine needles there lived a cross and sulky bear. Though everything around the bear- the tall pine trees, the honeycombs in the hollow oaks, the little white moths which danced prettily in the sunlight- was nice enough, still something made the bear sulky. She wanted something, but she did not quite know what. She sat with a sigh in the middle of the clearing and stared mournfully at her paws.

"Oh," she said to herself- not having anyone else to say it to- "I wonder what's WRONG." and she threw an acorn at a tree.

"I wonder if I want some fish," she thought, and she waddled out of the clearing down a little hill to the bank of the shining river. A fat and sleepy trout was hanging lazily in the water in the shade of the bank, but Bear didn't grab it out with her paw. "No," she said. "I'm not *hungry*." and she sighed again and sat down and thought. "Humph" And she wrinkled up her nose and sulked. "Growl."

by Sophy.

From Journal #80 (dated 1990)

My heart is a tree with wings

My heart is a tree with wings
I am hungry hungry for all
roots that drink of the damp earth
and branches flying to tomorrow

I am hungry, hungry for all
the river that suckles me streams
and branches flying to tomorrow
My sap remembers old stories well

The river that suckles me streams
into my roots. They sink deeper everyday
My sap remembers old stories well-
The song of continuing holds me, flows

Into my roots, They sink deeper every day
Against the flutter of my straining wings
The song of continuing holds me, flows
Familiar as I crave the sky.

From Journal 82, Sophia's last notebook. dated 4/8/96

What is self indulgence? The conviction that it is appropriate to alter one's moral code or go against one's better judgement, for the sake of immediate gratification. What is gratification? A sense that one's needs have been met. What is met? A temporal/physical and/or spiritual conjunction. What is conjunction? A joining together. What is together? Not alone. What is alone? Unaccompanied. What is unaccompanied? Without company, assistance, support or the presence of another. What is another? Not one. What is one? One is the loneliest number. What is a number? A symbol describing quantity. What is quantity? Either an amount of physical objects, a description of space or a characteristic, essential quality. What is quality? An index of comparison and value. What is value? A measurement or aspect of tone or brightness. What is brightness? Intellectual capacity. What is capacity? Ability or volume. What is volume? Degree of loudness. What is loudness? A garish clashing of mismatched styles or a brashness and abrasive aspect of personality. What is personality? Those aspects of one's public self by which one is generally known. What is known? Recognized and accepted as fact. What is fact? Data which withstands examination. What is examination? Challenging or critical scrutiny. What is scrutiny? Minute and detailed observation. What is observation? That period during which it is determined whether or not one requires psychiatric care. What is care? Tenderness and concern for the well-being of the person in question. What is question? To subject the status quo to examination and challenge. What is challenge? An extreme situation demanding performance at the highest, or heightened, level of ability. What is ability? Capacity to perform tasks or actions. What are actions? Illegal interruptions of oppressive governmental or military processes. What are processes? Those means by which any type of operation or series of operations takes place. What is place? The physical location of an event. What is an event? An instance or occasion of significance. What is significance? The degree of meaning generated by any particular action or occasion. What is occasion? That point in time in which an event takes place. What is place? To situate an object or person at a location; also to come second or third in a race. What is race? A strong, deep current in a stream or river. What is a river? A relatively narrow and deep body of moving water. What is water? A liquid consisting of a particular relationship between hydrogen and oxygen. THEREFORE self indulgence = water.

And when a girl

And when a girl
Has nothing to say, she
Writes anyway
Having the urge,
So to say.
Poor dear-
And young too-
It is always like that,
There's no curing it- the
Girl writes
Heavy words down rythmically
Purgatively
What will the neighbours say?
Oh they
Talk to,
When there's nothing else to do
They all
Stand and chatter and
Chatter and stand
And
When the poor dear
Ought to be working at something
Practical, she
Doesn't, she
Writes long poems down and carefully
Thinks, she
Writes thoughtfully and accasionally
Sucessfully
Being young.

us middle class

us middle class
   pretend to be poor
   dress up angry
   and finish school

   them puerto ricans
they're ruining the country
      lazy bastards
foreigners refuse good work

when i was a kid

well no you got to be liberal
   we have a great debt to repay
   the years of slavery
       and then they're so decorative

history honey well i mean we should be ashamed
      when you read the records
how we got our wealth
      but personal accountability is truly foolish

          i pledge myself to a new deal
        a great step for mankind
          give that nigger some grits
           but she can't come inside

am i supposed to explain
that i don't mean it
do i got to guilt trip my own self
honey SOME OF MY BEST FRIENDS...

do i got to choose between
   who i kiss
and what
     is the acceptable line on a currently trendy issue

us middle class
elipsis is the solution
i think I'll avoid that
confrontation

weary am I

weary am I and my heart is sad, hard-burdened with long woes
a song would I sing, song of dreary dull sorrows
plain plaint full of particular pity
drear is the life of low city

the cars rolling in ruinous herds, wild automatic animals
victorious they, their inanimate triumph, victors they in cement city
their springtide stampeding in the drab city
exaltation of leather and dirt and motion, and no pity

weary an I no place to rest, wandering wearily through dark alleys
traipse I tramp like no succour, urban, my heart is heavy
no buffalo but a big red bus

had I heart to dig down through dirt
piled for centuries on helpless valleys
then deep buried might I find
trace of fresh arbours, of sweet berries

gardens unmarxist but now we wallow
dragged doomwords by joyless high grey towers
through horrid expanses
without flowers

sorrow I for the systematic artificiality of urban sunshine
here walk we witless, we of the standard opportunity
sadness to bear we who have rationed joy
listen my love I will kiss your earlobe
this is an unparalleled act of resistance

joyous we in our separatist ignorance
forfeiting responsibility through selfish love
mad are the massed, we unmindful
suck love from a stone, my delight, on which we starve

incidence of violent crime comforts the criminal
who in his leather is for three seconds immortal
we of brevity doomed to levity
fly from fact, we are immoral-

laughter appears as a personal antidote
nos lacrimae rerum et ainsi de suite
it is I suppose easier to smile
than to carp, or weep

weary an I my heart is heavy
birds wing inevitably through spring air
romance and it's relation to season-
we are lice, my love, in the worlds hair.
and weary am I.

that she can have no worth but this

that she can have no worth but this
admission of coincidence,
not being herself wise-

how does an angry woman organize soirées?

married to a man whose
thoughts bred nurtured like
maggots on her worship, now
fat they are delectable and she a
shrine-keeper sings in
harmomy, attentively

how does she not see her pride?

where gabbling goodfolk swine
greedily giftgiving over her man
he sits in perfect order dressing
his words in nickering philosophy

who has held him in the dark
without a mind, how could he ignore his absence?
It wasn't there he was thinking man she
held him in some grey and dusty dark
suckling his sorrow with her time
she had no time, it was his entirely
a man cannot be asked to thank in absence
she smoothed his red hard rank shoulders after he
had hurt his soul inquiring into
matters of importance- her hands were hurting from
his sustenance but she had no self he lay on her moaning
whether she was his myth or his mistress,
always she held him in the dark she was
a vessel for his excess a balm a bandage she
lay under his crying soothing him an absence
you cannot ask a man to see who is lying under him,
she liked lying under him, she loved him
nevertheless a man has a life of his own (really
he had several lives, mostly they lay under him)

you cannot ask him for recongition a man is
really only a child a man
is busy and she did love him
so she lay under him. She held him in the dark.
an artist ascendent is given dinner by witty men an
ovation an entrecote she sits eclipsed and watches him
they worship him he rises over them like an angel
hot with wine, a flame thin with clarity, a
trumpet piercingly clear he talks and is heard and is seen
she blushing to him privately he sings a self ecstatic song

women in corners watch their works   their great achievements
graciously entertain   women in corners think proudly of the
succesful toys they've built   the boys around the bright table
clamor and shout, passing the wine
women in corners have no flesh of their own if they watch proud.

Oh my love

Oh my love
and oh my pink fleshed darling
and oh my most-unlike-a-ripe-strawberry woman,
whose love to me is like
the back of a white door at dusk
or any other seen thing to which
imagination give import-
do you think that we, victorian
in our transatlantic and
patient passion, who are not able
to share long looks, into the other's alien eye,
may have grown ritual
in the habits of love?

Who makes such an issue of
the impossibility of human intercourse
since we, in our wisdom exalted
(my name's wisdom, yours is glorious joy)
have to decided to discover that
individuality is also isolation, can
for longer than amusement kiss
conceptually, as though our lips
were aeroplanes?

You my anorectic sweet whose daily habit it once was
to eat and eat and eat then puke- I,
primate, privately preening, picking scabs-
we beasy monstrous, we intellect – who lie
once-in-a-blue-moon interwoven in
abstracts of romance-   well, I wonder:
"Is idle determination love?   Are we a hobby?"
(though not enough to change).

My Mother in a Small Plane

She's way up there now, man –
That Icarus he ain't
got nothing on her – more wings than
that Revelation's lamb,
more than the wildest saint -

I bet she's mocking them,
Mountains- they just think
they're the highest so damn
tall- but then, she's squashed them in one blink,

one laughing eye, one leap there,
right over them-
skimming the zip off clouds, air
splashing behind her, when
she herds the sky
she's breaking heaven's mare,

Busting it down – and hops
off; it's mild as milk
when she's done- no rope
tethers it; it slinks
crafty above her, but it can't escape.

“dilettante”

“dilettante”
accuses me.
I try to be
a sybarite
but somewhere deep
within the step
from sillines
to comedy
I met a physic
(remedy
to almost every
quiddity)
a secret sulphur
coarse and harsh
that cauterized
serenity
and made it seem
a reckless thing
to disregard
mortality-
and so I go,
a walking sign
of effort,
by it’s slow decline.

Sex: a love poem

Forms of address are dead, too slowed,
too thick and flat-
Something's hotter in the throat
and coarser in the eye
than what a voice reduces:

"We have an electric body. There is a charge-
a stunned flare 'round our breasts.
Moon cut us of white air-
We're glass, and spare and strange,
we're separate, or silent."

"I want a scar from you. Hard eyes are all
our blood; they tear our bodies, evidence
you stretch, pale, absent, to concussion.
Washing my face in your belly I burnt my hands,
I scorched them touching you. Is my mouth ash?"

Form of address are dead, too slowed,
a voice reduces love, or lust.
The burst of speech in final; while
a mind is wild it grows.

"Bodies are violent cities, never join
our borders char, the moon annihilates"

"I disappear, you're dark. The bliss.
Of changing silence. And our sweat."

Forms of address are dead, too slowed.
The voice reduces.

too much self control

too much self control
been bad for my soul
american kids
are myth addicts

we got a denim rebellion dream
saturday night
evil leather boys with the greased up hair
chewing gum seedy porn mags

i love an a&p supermarket
space out on commodities
laughing at the lemons and the
hygenic sugarhits

middle aged women
in the lime green leisure suits
high heeled white plastic shoes

in the movies you see that
bad assed boy
flaunting his groin
git down, eat popcorn

you ever had a wet dream for a chevrolet
fake leopard bucket seats
race away from the fuzz

you want to be king of the castle?
james dean is he irish or italian.
honey no history
but i could sell you a sweet horizon

(come on kiss me baby
you know you want
it)

mmm rock and roll
space patrol
democracy
means never having to say thank you

you boogie down in the wall to wall
makin out on the couch
my daddy sells bibles I want
your body

tv at 3 in the morning
coffee and coke
i never had no education but i like that
beat

white kids rampant in the dust they got
no particular conscience
it's a nuclear waltz at the edge of breakdown
us occidentals got to stick together

(come on kiss me baby
you know you
want it)

in morning come some sign

in morning come some sign
you love me yet- because lately
I don't dare
twist words

round to suit my-
what to call it- passion-

listen- this preoccupation with
the singleness
of particular selves- how I love *you*,
and *you* love *me*-
that sings
a rain stained green-misted glassy tepid shine,
faded and vain-

what I now hope for is a
justification of some kind-
a note we, as our single selves,
might strike on the abstract
for the sake and the use of generality:

love and the habit of love; our selves
as you and I, ourselves
as part of a motion, cells moving independently
to form co-ordinated wholes; our individual liberties
reacting together produce
love and the habit of loves: ourselves-
not private Romance,
just love, which happens
everyday, in the places we live
alone or loving each other, and
all of our separate strengths and failures-
us as ourselves,
me played faithfully by my self and you by you-
which show
what I would hope to call hope, for
every ordinary
waiting solitary

beautiful or ordinary
gentle and fierce beloved
grace woman given to possibility- the strength
that is us ourselves.

“when glorious in a first late denies . . .”

when glorious in a first
late denies our CHRISTIAN PERPETUALLY
PARTICULAR, and
succeed a reduces,
glorious mortal delays found
virgin, puritan touching pleasure.
Always kiss hard, be likely-
they (to bite)- joyous
can of, and can
to doubting sinner wet.

ii.
pleasure at day
the spite
beautiful, whip-tight,
too person saviour- body sing-
kiss self to full our perfect.
Of, likely, the word, our pagan wound
(most love promises fuller,
in at the stronger redemption) rejoice younger
quick our; and rewards
bring separate of good,
then to corporate,
specific:
we, feeling, sin.
But time, as dolor,
is expectant,
told selves prove...

iii.
when first christian
succeed mortal puritan,
kiss, they can, to pleasure-spite-
person self-perfect word
loves at younger rewards,
and separate,
to feelings as expectant

iv.
glorius late perpetually
delays
a touching
hard, too, of doubting
at beautiful saviour-body,

to pagan promises,
stronger,
quick being of corporate sin
and dolor told-

v.
in denies particular
reduces found pleasure
be biter and be sinner
be day and whiptight full

the likely wound is far fuller

redemption our laughter
better
and is specifically self

and glorious virgin
always likely
joyous can wet the too kiss, ours
is more in the rejoicing
and then
we prove
time sweet...

all madgirls eaten by their infancy

all madgirls eaten by their infancy
disfigured darlings knowing
only the poisons in education
will have their fevers and fears,
will have their times

all madgirls eaten by their girlhood
disown immediate time:
Oh Paradise cannot be far, if
Paradise is far the waiting's wearing.
There must be some faith
displayed, while waiting.

> "My own flower,"
> hums the dread tiger
> come to devour.

If there's no respite there's rest
but still   the garden seems threatening
Somehow an eagle's talon
grasps hard on the tight hot sun.

Oh Paradise can wait. Or be regained.
A brazen effort.

All madgirls eaten by worn patience
sigh in their elegance.
"When will it break me," they wonder
"or let me fade."

In precision there may be some ascetic breakthrough.
The forms which are indistinct in imagination must be escaped.
Struggle's the element to trust. But you must contain it.
It was a kind of guilded honesty it was
self-imitation, an exercise in personification.

> "My own flower,"
> hums the wan tiger
> but does not devour.

Oh aerialist- lover- unto thee

Oh aerialist- lover- unto thee
the rythm at last false play
(of stolen bases, all the way to third,
where comparison slides home to iniquity)
at last it falls to the pretty touching
of (never the same game in our grandparents' day)
the pause that refreshes.

Aerial and most inspired puppet
inspire, respire, expire, perspire but can the touch
expunge the lunge or quiet the beat of raindrops
falling and less distant
than the half-dreaming perfect buds of weep blooming
in the gardens of your eyes?
This is when the chin
can perforate the breath of a twilit belly
and impudent gaze travel the length
of a pleasant agnostic thigh.

Wet lips might bandage through the window
limp leaves of languid trees,
console them with the mixture of our souls.
Not so for cynics.
Hanging from gasping perches over some abyss of a mirrored death,
through which we fall and tumbling and fearful cry
(unless for the restraining victim's hand) for land.

your eyes which are so blue and laugh

Your eyes which are so blue and laugh
Sing loud and large
Of reeded rills and
Beckoning your white teeth like
Ivory forts
Shine amazing under lips
So soft and tender, lips;
What insubstantial, yielding gifts-

Your eyes which are so blue and laugh
While in places guarded by wary angels
(Gabriel guards us with Michael and their
Terrible swift swords like wings
Rush through the violent air)
We lie thigh to thigh and
Silent, beaming, while we
Pause and astonished peacefully shriek our prizes
Wide to encroaching Time...

Your eyes which are so blue and laugh
At vast flesh expanses as your
Fingers creep shivering to pieces tremulous fantasies
Your eyes
Delight and ravish;
Blue and impermanent
Skies.

What is there for the wandering egg head?

What is there for the wandering egg head?
Beautiful child, wingless
Of discrepancies and the Earth-Mother,
Roots damply in the soil of
Verisimilitude and hatching snobbery.

Futility, your married children,
Sons and daughters
Wander the earth grayly;
Regrets and promises
Fulfill their limitations
(Sigh and sigh,
Who was it in the fifth grade
Wrote the pretty sonnet,
Went on the gloried future
Of salesmanship and happy accountancy?)

Promises, wing-filled breaths of still-born angels,
Words grim before birth,
When the birth is a dying,
And the proud and endless hopes and fears
Of idolatrous mentors, worship
The crying flowers of poetry or grace
Foreseen in all, in withered innocent words
Uttered by all and thought by many
Until finally a time come when the mentors see
Pressed lilacs, tea-cakes, snap-shots and futility.

first published in the Putney Magazine, Fall, 1978

Roses.

Look, my love-
You walk between my pity and my anger.
And tread a narrow path.
(This is called love- a tenuous bridge of ropes,
This testament of hope
Above the jealous chasm of my harshness.)

Only look, my love-
My hand is on your neck and tries to guide
Your sure and careful footsteps
(Oh, this game demands too much:
Why must we weep
When you were made for laughter?)

This thing called love-
My love, do you plumb its depths?
Or is it shallow, sandbar where heron walks,
Eating my heart, Promethean,
Is it all shallow, fort against the surges
Of hostile deities and the flood of life?

Only look, love-
That rose I pulled from thorny bushes,
(That rose your heart)
And hold in the bleeding hollow of my palm-
Can I stay,
Or will it wither under my hot tears?

Love as I know it has only been allowed to be vague mixtures of imagination and the remoulding of what may have happened in the past depending on who has made or not made and broken or not broken promises that may not have been promises- love has been doubt left overnight to soak in a brew of stronger doubt, the whole thing breaded with flaky crumbs of impromptu and transitory hope... the power of invention combined with a bad memory and a shortage of belief produces so far as I can tell a permanent present, of which the future and the past are disconnected and impossible- memory through narrative becomes lies, no matter how much concrete evidence is available to support the conclusions drawn from experiences which are disqualified from faith by having been touched with the hindsight of later restatements of whatever hopes swam through the silly gauze of the Prime. . . I am old, I am young, I have finished, I become, I am wordy, I am dumb

Love love is an invention.

There once was a. . .a girl. She had red hair, and she sat in a bar, at the counter, facing the big red satin edged mirror, in which was reflected the room behind her, and her face. She studied her face as though she didn't recognize it, she knew she didn't recognize herself but had become accustomed to the stranger's face that stared at her wherever she stopped long enough to look... Her hair was short, her skin was grey pale and unhealthy, her expression that of one who no longer feels or fears the blows, unspecified, which when painful built the foundations of her incurable detatchment. She gives without effort the impression of timeless durability and a sort of undefeatible wish to be elsewhere which guarantees survival. The sour froth of the lager makes her purse her mouth pleasurably. She sits tensely, ready to jump up at the faintest hint of danger. Her name for the sake of convenience is Marion Medway and she is perhaps 25; she has lived for two years with a woman slightly older, one Hilda Wether. They are not and have not been happy together; it is incomprehensible, happiness, to Marion- she does not expect it, though she is under the impression that the painful questionings that she and Hilda put themselves through for the sake of a politically and personally and morally acceptable relationship will someday lead to peace and trust between the two of them- This she believes on principle, though she knows from the two previous relationships that ended painfully leaving her damaged and uncertain, that probably her relationship with Hilda will end having left behind a grainy residue that will serve to toughen the carapace, that will have taught her only a little more about "Life" than she could otherwise have learned- Marion is a woman full of doubts who expects and does not resent and converts to her own strength what she refuses to call failure-

She is sitting in the bar, it is naturally a gay bar, slowly with much thought drinking a lager. She has been alone for most of the evening and is glad to be so. When friends come into the bar, she nods without turning and either they notice the greeting in the mirror or they do not. Having most of them known Marion for some time, they can tell by the way she's sitting, that she doesn't want to be approached.

Earlier she had been with Hilda in the small apartment they share, a two bedroom flat with a shared kitchen and a bathroom on the landing. They live in a house owned by a sadistic drunken Irishwoman; most of the rooms are rented too expensively to students or other unemployed. Hilda has a job working in the mornings at a local library; Marion has no job, her parents send her an allowance so that she won't in some way embarrass them. Marion and Hilda often cannot stand each other. It becomes impossible for them to understand why they have for two years fought over the same immutable differences. Hilda becomes overcome with a feeling of helpless despair and sits silently at her desk staring down at the street; Marion gets furiously unbearably angry and walks around the town scowling until she comes to rest in the bar, where she drinks until the argument resolves itself into a pattern she can recognize calmly- then she goes home and she and Hilda love each other and have moments of optimism about the future.

Just now Marion has almost reached the point where she can feel drunk calm rising up about her legs, like a sweet grey mist and she stares at her reflection in the mirror with a rue-ful smile, considering herself a fool. The tiredness from her angry walking spreads pleasantly along her muscles, together with the dizziness lager. In the mirror she sees Helen, one of her oldest friends in the world, a very butch looking black woman, who laughs victoriously at everything. Shaking off her isolation, she turns around and smiles warmly.

now I know it ain't the sweetest way to sing this song of I'M A DYKE and I don't say as there ain't some of us who have got the whole thing taped, no prob, the future amazons engage in the conquest of autonomy, say n'more but there is also some of us, not I think a noticeable minority who have God forbid non-utopian relations with ourselves our lovers and the rest of the world; things are like up and down and it would be silly to lie. men are such assholes, how much do I believe in the rightness of revision in terms of a new-women's lidderatchyer? not much, not much.

THOUGH IT WAS early in the night, Maer was already anxious. He stared around the dirty backroom of Happy Joe's Cheap Good Food Restaurant with no concentration, letting his sight slide flexibly across the surfaces and colours it encountered without absorbing them. The room's appearance was, generally, blue. The lights in the corners were dimmed and obscured by blue glass cases that dropped thick intersecting shadows onto the room. The leather covers and the carelessly painted wooden walls of the four large booths were dark blue. The mirror on the wall against which Maer fidgeted his left shoulder reflected faint blue dusk and the shivering light on Maer's table. He stubbed out his cigarette in the blue glass ashtray and pushed the sliver fork idly through the gravy, in which could be seen shreds of old meat and a few lumps of unappealing mashed potatoes. Grits of coffee streaked the sides of the large clumsly white mug. Maer closed his eyes and leant back against the wall.

"Wake up, Maer."

"That you, Eyes?" Maer mumbled without opening his eyes or in any way appearing to move.

"Yes," said Eyes, sliding into the booth across from Maer, "You've eaten." Eyes took a piece of bread and mopped up the gravy with it, devouring it with indifference as he stared at Maer. He brushed the crumbs out off his Satan-suggesting beard. "Well, Maer. Mary and Charles are out back waiting in the car. Have you paid?"

Maer stood up impatiently and scowled at his reflection in the blue dusk of the mirror. Eyes, a tall thin black man, dressed in various browns and a sharp black hat looked up at Maer and waited. It seemed to my ear then, as it often did that friendship was nothing more than a group of misconceptions tolerating each other for the sake of convenience and advantage. He imagined what Eyes would look like when he was dead. He attempted to feel affectionate, and there seemed no other emotion suitable to the occasion. He smiled- Maer was unlovely but attractive; his face was long and pale and gave somehow, an impression of a private, powerful and disturbingly unreadable intelligence- and held out one long pale saintly hand to Eyes.

"Let's not keep them waiting, Eyes. You've all either eaten or got something to eat with you?"

Eyes nodded and got up. They went out the small back door, ducking along a dark low narrow hall and down a rickety flight of wooden stairs that creaked and shook under their feet as they hurried, feeling ahead with their hands in the dark. At the bottom of the stairs was a dark wood door with a window in it through which Maer saw the parking lot and behind that the low warehouses, docks, and the masts of yachts and fishing boats standing swaying in the dew-thick air. The moon was waning and was covered partly by a faint brown cloud. Light shone in the oily puddles of the parking lot, reflecting the angular doors and windows of deserted cars and the vans of the fish market next to Joe's. Mary and Charles sat in the front seat of Mary's huge red station wagon. Maer watched them smoking a joint against the small ceiling light. Eyes touched him impatiently on the shoulder and he opened the door. Eyes pushed past him and walked quickly across to the lot. Getting into the car as fast as he could. It was not very cold. Maer stood in the door for a moment staring up at the moon, but after a few minutes he shook himself and ran swiftly to the car. He struggled into the back seat next to Eyes.

"Pretty night, Maer," Mary said. Mary was one of Maer's few really close friends, one of the people he did not prepare himself for (one of the people for whom he did not prepare himself), with whom he felt only slightly ill at ease, they expected nothing of each other, but often extended remarkable generousities to each other, particularly extraodinary in view of their shared idea that nothing at all was reliable or durable except gullibility. Charles was her adopted younger brother, a tall, thin, shy, clever boy with glasses and a limp who said nothing and laughed at everything. He shook Maer's hand and introduced himself as though they hadn't met before because he was in love with Maer and angry at him for not reciprocating. But Maer for the sake of peace agreed not to be annoyed with his futile advances, so he ignored him with a smile.

"Beautiful," he agreed, resting his head on the back of the seat next to Mary, "Which Beach?"

First published in the Putney Magazine, Fall, 1978

THE ANARCHIST

Power-
The nexus of my converging lines,
It is not solid but a writhing mass.
Oh, for the lover and his lass
I wish, I wail and hope to see,
Hey ho, a marriage- not for me.
Observe my diverse winds-
They blow and struggle ragingly
And push, and pull, and tear in half
My ships, and sink them in the sea.

Oh lovelorn!
Hear the trumpets sound- An Armegeddon imminent-
And watch the angels scream and rush together,
All ancient, pagan and without their god
(for he has fallen)
Brandishing swords and weeping,
While beneath
Lord Lucifer leads satanic bacchanales.
Hear this, and know your grief
As minor discord in a fatal chaos

Not solid but a writhing mass.
This is the empty set, the so-called void
The brain pan of the knotted hairy ape,
And also mine. Look where the skies now wander
And fall in half, while we below
Stand deolate before the awesome grace
Of lifted
Power.

Motion Song

Give me a wagon to ride out my life
And horses to pull me up my hills,
A ream of paper to write it on
And godless men to sing it to.

Give me a carriage to jig out my life
A steeplechaser to leap the gaps
Some foolscap sheets to put it upon
And a crowd of christians to read it to.

Give me a Ford to drive out my life
And a horse to run my bets upon
A typewriter and some rolls of ink
And a group of critics to tell it to.

As for me
    joy boy con man cherrypicker, thief
as for me oh so sweetly impluverized youth
I do not digest
These same electrical impluses (which
in their certainty-of-egress
emitted sharply by the spiny-backed
red of hair-haze)
nor
    soldier beergut adulterer indian chief
confuse your sharp knife eyes
your flickering jittering snickering tongue
for the blue eyes
I stole, once, from innocence
or your
red triangular substitute
for that first-torn mouth

As for me, my biter bitterly bit
I scorn
the innuendo of your edible spine
refuse
the sly gossip of your smooth-skin bum
reject

the rumour of your silky inner knee
which you have said is open for discussion

not for worlds
not for truncated galaxies do I
perceive or impinge upon
the first eclipse of that
always diversly remembered
historic falsified night.

dated 27/4/79

Endless Song Unfinished

I say believe me woman and, again,
I say I have a reason
loving you is a sideways vision, and,
a walking-backward mystery
when the earth shines bright and now you see
I say I love you, when
I say I should cry and laugh
and turn around to see the sunset
or the pretty vicious moon;
hit me with a flower, and
I say turn to me, powerful,
I say with your melancholy body
and you gentle gentleness, I say
while I flame and touch you
with my hopeless hands, blind
I say I see you, silent,
Yet I know you fly away
with your bird-bones and your joy,
you go without me   woman
and I say
please learn to love me before
I say I'll say no more.

Ah, you may say it's all very well:

Ah, you may say it's all very well:
I do not
Relate sunstroke to beerbellies
(which you know
each evocative of a single
drivel-picture-)
Ah, but the long grass is
      the long leg is
the celebratorily   traditional
        oh-so-wedding-night is
so exquisitely upside down thanks to
SKILL
of the long necked witchdoctor (I or Thou?)
and conbubbled
conjoined
by a mutually exclusive inclusion
(Ha: a flatulent desirable dull HOT-BED
of   revision)

Which is afterwards expelled. By?
Oh I don't know. Malaria, say. Or
South-East Asia (in the long run).
Or you- my sweet strawberry tongued deceiver
in our Secret Observatory pitched on Planet X
for the intimate study of blue eyed denial-

Oh and then the whole unnecessary flowerstrewn waltz
is recommenced
in starlit nights
of? Heaven. Yes.

From Journal 81, dated 1992-1993

she had a reason

she had a reason to feel unreasoning
the reason was her reason was defined
by a desire to discover the abstract intensity of
pure knowledge
Which doesn't and can't exist in the face
of eternal and ceaseless change
her mind was full of questions and
her senses while deprived still yearned for
satisfaction she
held herself tightly together afraid afraid afraid
of the inexplicable vortices of energy which
surrounded her one day
she knew the next day she did not know
and then she knew again
there was a cycle there was a pattern
the pattern was randomness she thought she
should try not to think she thought and
thought about not thinking
she ascended to
a state of grace and then removed herself
from herself so utterly that only a panic of the
most monstrous kind could restore her to her
body
and when she had plummeted back out of
metaphysics and into her body
she was so confused and revolted by the earthiness
and fundamental mortality of her condition that
once more she resorted to thought as an analgesic
analysis and hairsplitting
she flayed herself alive for not achieving perfection
she flayed herself for flaying herself and then
she laughed at the paradox
her body rejoiced for a moment there was victory
of the senses and of survival as she realized
her mind could not dictate her experience her mind
could react and affect it but life itself was a
flooding river and she was not a leaf floating

separate upon its surface but one of an uncountable
number of molecules of water absorbed and carried
forward by a spate whose source and end were and
are unknowable she imagined a molecule of water
trying to evaporate itself through willpower and laughed
again at the intensity of her own stubbornness
but still she feared the velocity of the flood which
contained her.
she wanted to know the nature of her relationship
to everything around her which as she analyzed it
did not become but appeared and felt more and
more tenuous-
another paradox to be frightened at the feeling that there
is no feeling she felt herself detaching and becoming
isolated.
she was afraid to lose her identity she was afraid to
declare her identity she was afraid to see all parts of
herself as they really were
she wanted life's river to love her and she wanted to
love the river back- she was
attracted and terrified by the unconscious energy and
irresistable power of something beyond her control
she could not decide whether to submit or resist
to surrender or merely survive.
she desired and felt both conditions equally
she longed lustfully to be overwhelmed and carried away
To surrender responsibility and as a consequence to surrender
being blamed
but she was afraid of annihilation.
her trust was very very small but still despite herself her
spirit grew and grew she resisted and delighted in
this growth this expansion and finally beyond her control
she burst and became ether
essentially involved in all things
fundamental level of matter but also fluid and
transparent
she was a part of life's breath and had no fear
as she hurtled forward into a future as fragile and
resilent as her own senses and perceptions
all things around her changed constantly and she
changed with them and around them she changed

them as she passed through them and they changed
her she was a current of wind moving upon the
waters of breathing rythm of motion and creation
she felt her own lungs expand and fill with the
explosive and ineffable power of life
all life is change she shouted at the top of her lungs
all change is life
all things become one another gradually or swiftly all
things merge weave and unweave themselves governed only
by chance on a basic level
the stuff of life is miracles
she looked at herself at her reflection on the moving
waves of the enormous river and saw that she was a
strange new angel that she had never seen before
she marvelled at the new power of her feathered wings
she felt gratefully the elastic grace of her electrified
muscles and nerves she was a stranger to herself but
delighted by the discovery of her beauty
and a little afraid out of habit that it might not
last
she lifted her wings upon the wind and was borne
up whether she moved or lay still she was borne
effortlessly along
even the air around her was full of tenderness and
forgiveness
she saw that nothing in itself is evil
the source of evil is fear the source of pain is fear
the source of everything that had ever assailed her
pure delight in the constant detonation of change
all around her was fear
and fear blew away upon the wind till only light
filled her heart her mind and her mouth
she was a crystal permeated with every color of light
she knew her birth in everything she saw
she felt her flesh in everything she saw
all that she knew or could know was change and
faith
her hands were opened wide- in each palm she
saw the painting of an eye opened wide to
remind her that she must see and know with all
her being- her mind and her grace were in her

soul which filled every part of her body
thought was far from the only form of knowledge
available to her
she reached out to either side and her arms were
filled with love
she saw she was flying above the river still and
around her on every side and above and below
were a myriad of angels of every kind
who meant her no harm
who were as she was carried along by the wind of
joy that echoed in the air like music
she flew and flew for as long as she lived an
angel of change constantly assuming new forms
and accepting and releasing those forms as she
went into and came out of them
she learnt with every part of her and as she learnt
her voice and power grew till all of her body was solid
and replete with satisfaction
she was not afraid she was protected she was loved and
she loved others
she took pleasure in her true self and hid nothing
even when she didn't understand herself she was

(last page ripped out)

listen

listen to the beginning hiss
across the mist

see the bold fog roll across
the road

two days more and elegance
will dine with pride

no more no more the meaning
is denied

is denied its fruit, its purpose, its purchase
the meaning slips as slick as slime
across wide expanses

dances

do you know the way to be the way to
be the way to be?

Who can hold the opening in an absence
of center?

listen to the beginning hiss
translations of its own maloccludedness
across the spitting pits of
crisping bliss

burnt ecstasy
charred love.

you are wide

you are wide and I am in the way of
your entrance, entranced
I stand across the gap of
intermittence- do you traverse
the collapsible planes of absence?
I command your presence, I tell you stories
to which you may not listen-
what is it about you?
You are an empty field, I am a haggard sheep,
and I will feast upon your meager grass
you will feast upon my festive tongue
we will feed language to the rivers of the world
and words of water will want rewards
for sounding wet, sibilant, superlative-
you are narrow, a twin lock but I am not a
key, I butt frustrated against a
whole too small
can I call you at home?
my trumpet will summon the last ashes of creation
you are the queen of being, I am no peon
what? sensibilty is derived from peace-
I desire surcease
let my long lips linger lovingly upon thee
sweet astonishment converts to a release
I tell you again I summon angels with a word.

dated 1/4/93

A CONVERSATION IN THE KITCHEN

afterwards/words
speech fills up the lips it
slips softly across flesh and
flows rich over teeth and
tongues while eyes
wet orbs rotate
in their bone caverns and
the mind finds light and
form with which to make
exchange   how strange
the range of space traversed
by sound projected from
these simple bodies
still I know or trust an
echo will result from effort
you are there I see you
if I reach and touch my skin
will tell me I have felt
the edges of your shape and
presence/essence will amaze:
the fact and mystery of living
together- all the other things   in the room
are there too everything is
there at the same time
and here we are

dated 2/19/93

A LAMENT FOR BIRDS WHICH ARE DEVOUR'D

TELL ME AGAIN
HOW THE HEN
MADE FRIENDS
WITH MEN

HOW HER SHORT WINGS
WERE STRIPPED
HER FEATHERS CLIPPED
HER WHITE FLESH DIPPED

IN BOILING WATER
HEY! THE SMALL DAUGHTER
OF EARTH AND SKY, THEY CAUGHT
HER
AND TAUGHT HER
SLAUGHTER

TELL ME ONCE MORE
OF HOW THIS WAR
WAS WON- THE POOR
BIRD LIVES NO MORE

THE TRUSTING BIRD
LOOKS UP WITHOUT A WORD
I HAVE NEVER HEARD
IF SHE PREFERRED
BEING SIMMERED OR STIRRED

HER SMALL HEART
SILENCED PLAYS NO PART
ONCE THE CHEFS START
TO WORK THEIR TASTY ART

WHAT I WOULD LIKE TO LEARN
IS WHEN IT WILL BE OUR TURN
TO EARN
THE RIGHT TO BURN

THESE PRETTY BEASTS
KILLED QUICKLY BECOME FEASTS
AS SOON AS THEY HAVE CEASED
TO BREATHE- THE LEAST

WE CAN DO IS TRY
AS OFTEN AS POSSIBLE TO REMEMBER
WHY

WE WOULD WANT TO FRY
A TRUSTING BIRD THAT CANNOT FLY

WHEN WE PICK OUT OF OUR TEETH
THE LAST FIBERS OF THEIR DEATH
RECALL THEIR LIVELY BREATH
IS WHAT WE EAT

TELL ME AGAIN
HOW THE HEN
MADE FRIENDS
WITH MEN

THIS BETRAYAL
LIKEWISE OF PIDGEON AND QUAIL
WREN, PARTRIDGE, TEAL-
AN UGLY TALE.

-FINIS-

WE HAVE BECOME THE THICK DARK ROOT OF SILENCE I TOLD YOU TODAY IN THE MORNING WHEN I SAW THE BRISTLING SOFT FELT OF THAT UNFAMILIAR BOWLER HAT BALANCED AGAINST THE PALE VULNERABLE ROSES OF YOUR BUTTOCKS- I WHISPERED IT SO SOFTLY IT WAS A SHOUT THAT SHOOK THE LEAVES OFF EVERY TREE FOR MILES BUT STILL YOU DID NOT SEE ME- I HAVE SURPRIZED MYSELF BY BECOMING A GHOST- THERE IS NO SUBSTANCE TO ME- I AM A DISCRETE CONCATENATION OF ABSENCES, UTTERLY TRANSPARENT AND LOVELY- YOU SEE RIGHT THROUGH ME- AND YOU DID NOT HEAR ME, EVEN WHEN I SANG- NO ROOSTER'S COARSE ERUPTIVE CRY, NO SOLEMN CHANT, MERELY THE EXQUISITE BRIEFNESS OF A BIRD'S EXPERIMENTAL CALL- I TELL YOU SECRETS AND YOU DO NOT KNOW- NEITHER DO I- I DECEIVE MYSELF AS THOROUGHLY AS I MISLEAD YOU- TONIGHT WHEN THE TINY MOON HANGS MINIATURE AMONG THE TREMBLING STARS MY BREATH WILL ECHO AT THE NAPE OF YOUR NECK; YOU'LL TURN TO FOLD ME INTO YOUR STRONG, LEAN, HARD, PALE, GRACEFUL ARMS BUT THEY WILL MEET ON EMPTINESS- ONLY MY EYES, HANGING ALONE IN MID-AIR, WILL ANSWER YOUR STARTLED STARE- AND THEN WITH SADNESS, QUESTIONS, RANDOMNESS, UNCERTAINTY- STILL, WHILE YOU SLEEP, MY LIPS PERHAPS MAY YET MATERIALIZE- RED, WARM, HUGE, SOFT- AND <u>SUCK</u>, YEARNING, THE TIGHT BUDS OF YOUR HARD NIPPLES- SALTY RASPBERRIES, SMALL SOFT STONES MELTING AGAINST THE WET HEAT OF MY SEARCHING TONGUE. BUT IF YOU WAKE, REACH OUT, AGAIN IT WILL BE SUBSTANCELESS AIR YOU STRIVE TO TOUCH- THE LAST TREMORS OF MY FADING VOICE CARRIED RAPIDLY AWAY AS YOU, BEWILDERED, SEARCH EVERYWHERE AROUND YOU- BUT ONLY WHEN YOU DO NOT SEEK ME AM I HERE

THE LIES THAT MOTHERS TELL THEIR DAUGHTERS

THE LIES THAT MOTHERS TELL THEIR DAUGHTERS
THE LOVE THE DAUGHTERS FEEL, THE HATRED
CAUGHT IN THE AXIS POINT BETWEEN DISTRUST AND TRUST
REMEMBERING FROM MANY POINTS OF VIEW
THE SHALLOW SAFETY, THE DEEP DANGER UNDER IT

THOSE MOMENTS WHEN
OUT OF THE STIFF STALKING SILENCE COMES
A RECOGNITION
YOU ARE A WOMAN IN THE CENTER OF HER OWN LIFE
I AM A WOMAN FINDING THE CENTER OF MINE
STRANGERS
DECIDING FOR AN INSTANT TO ADMIT
THE REASONS FOR THE CHAOS ALL AROUND US
WE HAVE NOT CHOSEN IT
IT DOES NOT DISTINGUISH US
IT HAS BEEN DONE TO US
AND YOU HAVE DONE IT, ALSO, DONE IT TO ME

THE LIES THE MOTHERS TELL THEMSELVES THAT
END IN DAUGHTERS' TERROR
WITH NO TRUTH TO HOLD TO FIRMLY
WE CLIMB THE SLIPPERY ROCKS OF WHAT WE SEE
AS THEY DISSOLVE UNDER US-
IF WE HAD NAMED THEM, IF YOU HAD NAMED THEM
WE COULD HAVE CLIMBED OVER THEM

THE LIES THAT MOTHERS TELL. ECLIPSING US COMPLETELY
TO PRESERVE A FRAIL SENSE OF PROPRIETY
WHEN I CAME SCREAMING BLOODY OUT BETWEEN YOUR THIGHS
YOU SHOVED ME HARD IT HURT US BOTH WHEN WE FIRST MET, OUR EY
THE EYES OF STRANGERS LOOKING COMPLETELY NEW AT ONE ANOTHEF
MOTHER
WAS MY FRAGILITY WORTH LESS THAN WHAT CAME BETWEEN US?

THE LIES THAT MOTHERS' MOTHERS TOLD THEM, PASSED ALONG-
WE HUDDLE TOGETHER AS FROM A CYCLONE WHILE
OUTSIDE THE FATHER AND THE HURRICANE, THE FOOL,
THE MAN WITH AN AXE TO GRIND, THEY ALL

WHIRL AND DESTROY, WHIRL AND DESTROY, OUTSIDE OUR SCOPE
OF ACTION- IT HAS BEEN DONE TO US-
WE DO NOT MENTION IT- WE HUDDLE TOGETHER
AND SAY
WE ARE NOT COWERING- WE DON'T DESCRIBE, EXPLAIN, PREVENT-
THE CONSEQUENCES OF DESCRIPTION:
NOTHING WILL REMAIN AS SHELTER

THE CONSEQUENCES OF SILENCE:
RAGE, CONDENSED TO POINTS SO FINE AND HOT
THEY PIERCE THE SKIN INSTANTLY, UNOBSERVED,
AS TINY VENGEANCES PLAYED OUT AGAINST
THE FLESH OF CHILDREN
THE MOTHERS WITH THEIR SILENCED THROATS
DESCRIBE DESTRUCTION WITH THEIR HANDS
AS THEY ATTACK THE DAUGHTERS-

THE RAGE WITH WHICH THE DAUGHTERS VIEW OUR MOTHERS
NOW THAT WE KNOW THEIR SAFETY WAS A LIE
HOW COULD THE BODY-KNOWLEDGE BE LOST SO FAST THAT COMES
FROM MY HEAD PUSHING THROUGH THE STRETCHING OF YOUR CERVIX
MY ELBOW CAUGHT AT AN ANGLE IN YOUR WOMB
A MAN REACHES IN AND TURNS MY HAND AGAINST YOU
YOU YELL FROM YOUR DEEPEST SELF AND STRAIN
I SLIP WAILING OUTSIDE YOU

A poem given to a friend.

Some Maps and Stories

I want to tell you a story about my hands:
a group of bones and muscles made for touch,
covered with finely whorled skin
that sings like an antenna in
anticipation

I want to try and tell you about your shoulders
and the palms of my hands
splayed out across the strength of your
long back,
my strength meeting your strength
flowing down together in a
multitude of currents to pool
in shadows at the curve of your spine-

to tell you about my gaze
travelling lazily around you
slicing precisely through hot air of distance: thy eyes
tell me stories about your collarbone, its long straight lines;
your thighs which have metered the rhythm of my breathing;
the dark cinammon star cresting the soft curve of your belly
as you move

I need to tell you a story about the things I
haven't said and haven't done because
I'm just too damned polite: a story without words
as parts of yourself meet with parts of myself
and we roll inside an echo of recognition-
about our bodies touching; the kind of story a
river would tell as it wore through a dam,
deep currents carving into river bed
under the silent surfaces, under stillness-
about passion and patience and how sometimes they're the same thing

How my teeth wait for the curve of your neck
because they know
the smell, the touch, the taste, already-
how teeth and tongue and saliva will
meet your skin

It's a story of travelling slowly and steadily
towards a destination, enjoying
the route as much as the goal,
knowing sweet details of the voyage
make the moment of arrival
all it is

I've made a map, and carry it with me:
how to travel up the back of your thigh from the
sweet oasis of your knee- to explore
the range of your spine even as
plate tectonics on the dense plane of your back
shift and regroup you, shift and regroup me-

Another map for you to take when you want it:
somewhere to rest for a while, where touch
(my voice, my breath, my hands and mouth)
will tell you long stories about your body, where
passionate mirrors/my eyes will show you
electric glimpses of yourself, reflected in varying light-
where a continuous rhythm of deep knowing
will rock you
until you nccd to lcavc
where fluttering hands will wing you into peace,
hard hands will lift you into tomorrow,
open hands hold and release, hold and release-

The following piece was found in Sophia's last journal, no. 83.

^ahem^

It's a question of really enjoying a certain way you laugh
That makes me wonder how much I can ask of my nerves-
It's a sensuous thing, and I know just how much it satisfies
Me- am I ready to know you see it in a different light?
I know I'm ready when you're dancing in your blue pyjamas,
Reckless and whirling- it's when I'm alone I have my doubts-

It's an ambivalent kind of seduction when we're both so full of doubts.
Sometimes I think you trust me the most when you hear my ironic laugh.
Here I am lying in bed with a cold, bundled up in drab pyjamas,
Wishing that wanting to touch you didn't put such a strain on our nerves,
Earnestly writing a love poem, but trying to keep it light;
Hoping I'll reach you with something gentle that still satisfies.

You know how much I want to find whatever it is that satisfies
You- Here I am trying to please, still full of passions and doubts-
It's funny to see how beautiful you are, the way it lights
Me up inside 'til just looking at you I want to laugh
With pleasure. Still, at the same time, I'm vibrating with nerves,
As if I were a guitar and you strummed me, sprawling back in your blue pyjamas.

I want to respect your boundaries, I want to unbutton your pyjamas-
Would it be my hand that satisfies your skin more, or your skin that satisfies
My imagination? Can you imagine what it does to my nerves,
Wondering if I should listen more to my hopes or our doubts?
Really I'd rather listen to you laugh,
Listen to you sing, as your voice moves back and forth from dark to light-

Really I'd rather just sit somewhere with you in the sunlight,
Bring you a cup of tea while you laze about in your pyjamas,
Share the calm and quiet, and if it happens, laugh

At some quirk of the day- to try and deliver what satisfies
You, by any means possible. Shouldn't we put aside our doubts?
I think we might enjoy kissing- sometimes nerves
Exist purely to perpetuate generations of new nerves.
I don't want a romantic drama from you, I want a light
Flower of physical friendship- Certainly, listen to your doubts,
but then, please, take off your pyjamas:
I think *that's* how to find what satisfies-
Let me try to find your most sensual laugh.

The kind of nerves that come from unbuttoning blue pyjamas for the first time
Those are the ones that satisfy- in dark or in daylight,
Let's lay down our doubts, lie down together, laugh.

much love-
Sophia

From Journal 81, dated 1992-1993

SLEEP NO MORE YE HUSSIES

SLEEP NO MORE YE HUSSIES SLEEP NO MORE
AWAKE AND SPY BEHIND THE KITCHEN DOOR
FOR THEREIN GROWETH A VASTY LEMON TREE
DESPITE THE LACK OF SOIL AND WATER- SEE
HOW DEEP WITHIN THE WHITE CERAMIC TILE
THE ROOTLETS PUSH THEMSELVES FOR MANY A MILE-
REMARK THE HORSE THAT EATS THE LEAVES THEREOF
HER EYES ARE WEEPING BLOODY TEARS OF LOVE-
FROM OUT HER ECHOING THROAT A LUSTY SONG
WAVERS FROM STOVE TO TREE ALL SUMMER LONG
HER SHRIEKING WHINNY PIERCES E'EN THE SKY
AND 'NEATH HER TEATS THE FAINTING PONIES LIE-
SUCKING HER MILK BETWEEN THEIR SIGHING YAWNS
THEY MUTTER SLEEPILY OF UNICORNS
AND SADLY DREAM THAT SOMEDAY THEY WILL WAKE
AND GORGE THEMSELVES ON PILES OF RASBERRY CAKE.
MEANWHILE THEY LIE AND DRINK OF DRUGGED MILK:
THEIR HOOVES ARE DIAMOND AND THEIR MANES ARE SILK
THEIR VERY COATS ARE VELVET AND THEIR LIPS
ARE SOFT WHEREON THE MILK OF STILLNESS SLIPS-
THREE HORSES, THEN, BEHIND THE KITCHEN DOOR-
BUT MARK, HOW STRANGE THE SUBSTANCE OF THE FLOOR!
A BLACK AND WHITE PATTERN OF BROKEN TILE
FOR UNSUSPECTING EYES A DEVIOUS TRIAL
FOR EVERY DAY IT CHANGES- FIRST FROM CLAY
TO RINDS OF MELON- ON THE FOLLOWING DAY
THIS ROTTING FRUIT
TRANSFORMS TO SHIMMERING ICE
WITHIN WHICH FREES THE LIMBS OF HELPLESS LICE
AND THEN IT MELTS, BECOMES A MUD SO THICK
WITH BERRIES FAUNS AND DRYADS COME TO LICK
SOFT FRUIT FROM OFF ITS SURFACE- WHILE THEY EAT
THE COOLING MUD BECOMES A SATIN SHEET
STREWN WITH ALL SORTS OF GEM- WITH EV'RY KIND
OF JEWEL T'ENTRANCE THE LIGHT BEDAZZLED MIND-
THEN MANY SWOON WHO WITNESS THIS EXTREME
OF OPALESCENT, GEM SET, RUBY DREAM

THEY LIE ALL FAINTING 'CROSS THE KITCHEN FLOOR
HEAPED BY THE STOVE AND STACKED UP BY THE DOOR.
THIS IS BUT ONE OF ALL THE FANTASIES
THAT SAIL ACROSS THIS KITCHEN'S CHANGING SEAS
HERE BY THE SINK SEE HOW THE GOLDEN VINE
AROUND THE SILVER FOUNTAIN DOES ENTWINE
ITS MINUTE TENDRILS WHILE DREAD ICY BIRDS
SHOUT TO THE DISH RACK TERRIFYING WORDS
THAT CHILL THE BLOOD AND SPEAK OF AWFUL DEEDS-
AND HERE BENEATH THE TOASTER GRASS AND WEEDS
COMBINED TO FORM A PLAIN OF SUCH EXPANSE
WITHIN IT DWELLS THE GREATER PART OF FRANCE:
IN MINIATURE THE TINY PEOPLE SPEED
ACROSS THEIR NATION, LIVE AND DIE AND BREED
LIKE GALLIC MICE, WHILE IN THE KITCHEN/SKY
SLOWLY REVOLVES THE HARSH BUT PATIENT EYE
FROM WHICH ALL LIGHTNING COMES- ITS SPARK
ANNIHILATES BEFORE IT LIFE AND DARK
IT STRIKES WITH SPEEDY FLAME THE MARBLED SHELVES
WHEREON DO COWER AND GAMBOL BITTER ELVES:
THEIR CYNICAL SONG RISING FROM AMONG
WHERE PLATES ARE STACKED AND COFFEE MUGS ARE HUNG.
THEY SNEER AND LOOK ACROSS THIS MYTHIC ROOM
WITH MOST UNELFLIKE ANOMIE AND GLOOM.
BUT IF YOU ASK THEM THEY WILL ONLY SAY
"OH THINK IT OUT YOURSELF- NOW GO AWAY!"
IN PIPING VOICES AS THEY CAST THEIR DARTS
STINGING AS HORNETS TOWARDS OUR TRUSTING HEARTS
THUS CHASTENED WE RETREAT AND WISELY FLEE-
MOUNTED PERHAPS UPON A GIANT BEE
WE HUM THROUGH CLOUDLESS AIR AND, LANDING FIND
WE HAVE BEEN RENDERED TEMPOR'LY BLIND,
DAZZLED BY MIRROR'D LIGHT THAT BOUNCES BACK
FROM IRON BURNERS POLISHED SHINING BLACK
AND GLEAMING WITH THE GLOW OF LEAPING FLAMES
THAT SPRING FROM GAS-JETS- HERE HAS BEEN BARELY TAMED
A FIRE WHICH MIGHT BURN ALL, AND YET DOES NOT
(ALTHOUGH AT TIMES IT IS EXTREMELY HOT)-
AND HERE ABOVE THESE BURNERS EVER FRY
DINNERS THAT COOK ALIVE AND NEVER DIE:
FISH CRYING MERCY, CHICKEN PEEPING SHRILL

STEAK COOKING SLOWLY AND AGAINST ITS WILL.

WHAT CAN YOU USE INSTEAD OF WORDS? I HAVE ALWAYS WONDERED. HORSES EATING LEAVES OFF THE TREES, HORSES GETTING GAS FROM EATING WINDFALL FRUIT- TODAY THE PURPLE TREE WAS FAT WITH RAIN- I SAW KAREN ACCIDENTALLY SHE WAS NAKED AFTER HER SHOWER TALL AND LITHE AND PALE BENT OVER IN A LOVELY CURVE STEPPING INTO HER TROUSERS SHE IS BEAUTIFUL SO MANY WOMEN ARE BEAUTIFUL. THE TELEVISION BELLOWING GARBAGE I NEED SOME DREAMS I NEED SOME RAMPANT ROSES IN THE PURPLE DUSK I NEED BLUE MULES WHINNYING IN THE RAIN I NEED THE SLOW GROAN OF ENORMOUS SNAILS PROCEEDING SEDATELY ACROSS THE MOONLIT PAVEMENT I NEED A MOUTH AS HUGE AS A HOUSE WITH LIPS AS RED AS LIPSTICK AND SLICK WITH THE SALIVA OF A MUSCULAR TONGUE THE SIZE OF TWO HORSES I NEED TEETH LIKE MAUSOLEUMS THE DARK CAVERN OF MY ECHOING THROAT FULL OF THE DEEP HOWL THAT WILL EXPLODE ACROSS INVOLUNTARY SILENCE LIKE A SILVER STREAM OF MOLTEN STEEL- I NEED A SHOUT THAT WILL STUN ENTIRE STADIA ALL AT ONCE- I WILL ARISE FROM MY DIM SLEEP WHICH HAS MADE ME THINK I AM NO DIFFERENT FROM THE QUIET HILLS, I WILL ARISE SHAKING OFF MY BLANKET OF SHAKING TREES AND GROANING ASSUME MY MONUMENTAL STANCE I WILL BE A STONE WOMON HEWN FROM ROCKS AND EARTH MY LIMBS WILL FREE THEMSELVES FROM STRANDS OF ROOTS AND FILAMENT, SNAKES WILL FALL WRITHING AWAY FROM MY SUDDENLY REVITALIZED MUSCLES, SMALL AVALANCHES WILL SHAKE LOOSE FROM MY EYES AND THIGHS, MY OPENING HAND WILL RELEASE BREEZES THAT FLATTEN THE GRASSES AND SING HUMMING AMONG THE BRANCHES OF THE HUDDLING TREES THE MOON AND I WILL TRADE IMPASSIVE STARES AS ICE COLD WATERFALLS SPRAY OFF MY HIPS- I WILL PROCEED IMPLACABLY ACROSS ALL VAST TERRAINS EACH STRETCH OF UNINHABITED WILDERNESS WILL BE MY FOOTPRINT AND WHERE I STEP

THE WIDE SANDY PATH LINED WITH WILD ROSES- THE SOFT ORANGE BULBS OF ROSEHIPS AND THE THIN THORNY VINES SPREADING ACROSS AND OVER THE WIDE SANDY PATH- BERRIES TOO THAT WE PICKED IN PASSING LEANING OUT INTO THE BRAMBLES BALANCING ON THE SANDY STONES THAT SHIFTED

GRITTY UNDER OUR HARD BARE FEET- THE WIDE SANDY PATH WITH DARK GROWTH ALL ABOUT IT FULL OF THE BLUE SMELL OF SEA- DOWN ALONG THE PATH (IT WAS A SHORT, FAT PATH) WE SAW THE CHOCOLATE COLORED SAND IN STREAKS AGAINST THE PALER SAND- THE STEADY ROWS OF LOW SMALL WAVES BREAKING STEADILY AGAINST WET GREY SAND- THIS WAS THE OLD PEOPLE'S BEACH, QUIET SMALL AND SLOW, FAR AWAY FROM OUR HOUSE, WHERE ALL THE RICH OLD COUSINS LIKE WATTLED LIZARDS CAME OUT TO SUN THEMSELVES, HARDLY MOVING IN THE MILD WARM LIGHT- THEY WERE SO OLD, SO LEATHERY, THEIR VOICES HARSH WITH CIGARETTES- WE STARED AT THEM UNBELIEVING, HALF PROUD AND HALF AFRAID TO HEAR THEY WERE OUR OLD, OLD COUISINS- WE SEEMED SO TINY NEXT TO THEM- I SPIED, RUNNING PAST, PRETENDING NOT TO LISTEN, HOPING TO HEAR SOME CLUE: THEIR VOICES WERE SO DEEP, THEIR SUNGLASSES SO DARK- THE OLD DROOPING GREY HAIRED BREASTS OF THE MEN, THE THIN LIVER SPOTTED HANDS OF THE OLD WOMEN, THEIR RUBBER SANDALS FLAPPING SOFTLY AS THEY STEPPED ACROSS THE SAND AND STONES- THAT GREY, OLD, SMALL AND QUIET BEACH, FULL OF THEIR ARROGANCE, THEIR RICHNESS- THE WIDE FLAT STRETCH OF SAND, THE SLOW FLAT STRETCH OF BARELY MOVING SEA- THE MYSTERIOUS COUSINS WARMING THEIR OLD BLOOD AND ALL ALONG THE PATH THE BLOODY SWELLING RED OF ROSEHIPS AND SWEET BERRIES

dated 3/18/93

EVE RECALLS AN APPLE THAT GAVE PLEASURE TO HER

I saw two apples on a tree
and neither one was meant for me
but still I reached and still I ate
and ever after faced my fate
the leaves as green as all leaves are
as diamond bright, as lustrous, sharp
curled round the hard red fruits of war,
the small red worlds- no angel's harp
sang out in warning as I stood
naked along beneath the branch
or as I reached up- red as blood
they were- and chose one sphere by chance-
I bit into the dewy flesh
and echoes yet throughout my soul
the sudden startling frightening fresh
delight that to my taste did fall
I stood, and shivered in the wind
merciless made separate
by this awakening of the mind,
by this hard fruit that feeds me yet-
I saw two apples on a tree
and neither one is meant for me
but still I reach and still I eat
and still my senses flood with heat
and ever and again I find
the lonely ecstasy of mind.

A silence of Shorn tongues

A silence of Shorn tongues, a silence of stillborn souls oh no oh no bloody stumps of clipped muscle shiny with spit and blood pulsing blue fat artery beneath it with its artificially violent opening pouring out dark blood the sound of pain the stumbling inarticulate scream the mixture in that sound of terror and confusion who took the cold edge of steel to this fat stump? Who pressed a cleaver to this hurting muscle, who reached into the complex cavern of the mouth, behind the wet white fortress of the teeth and sliced the source of speech from off its root? Who could be so sudden and unkind? How having a tongue themselves also could anyone perform this furious and hateful surgery upon another? And who having had their precious broad soft muscle, wet, strong, sensuous, unconscious and capricious and delightful- who having had this lifelong source of satisfaction, sex and mystery sliced off could understand it, ever? The eyes must widen, blue broad blasted til so much light comes in that images are meaningless- it is a betrayal of the fundamental kind which robs all following experience of any sense.

test the tenses

test the tenses of invention
never mention your intention
to cement the declension
of their surface tension

seek always for the sleek
avoid the chic
flee pique

so many hens peck when
the bubbles of suffering burst
remember to dismember terror first
let long breaths of life belief live blissfully upon the earth

question the ingestion of fustian principles
digest the least detail of voice
choose the challenge of cheap peace and
wade in the water of willing simplicity.

In front of the train station two boys throw snails into a wheelbarrow. Sam is the smaller- he is frail but wily, an ugly, charming, skinny survivor. his cousin Angus is less ephemeral and less intelligent. They are both bored. it is the middle of the day. Across the tracks at the ferry dock the boats let out the mournful shrieks of their sirens as they pull slowly into the harbor. Angus rode across to the island with their grandmother once. Sam's envy is intense but disavowed. He jeers at the boats, at their wide unwieldy iron decks, at the huge screws of their propellers churning into the flat, oily water. Angus smiles, smug, and says nothing. Above it all the wheeling seagulls arc and dive, mewing and calling. Bending down to pick up a huge, tan colored snail- it must have been brought out by last night's rain- Sam notices he can look from under the barrow up the skinny legs of a girl standing on the opposite platform. He smiles. He won't tell Angus. The snail makes a satisfying clatter, rattling against the metal sides of the barrow. Angus is daydreaming with a snail in one hand, watching the seagulls circle overhead. The air smells briny, from the thick brown kelp washed up against the docks. Sam bends down again as if to pluck a snail off its wet track and stares with curiosity at the white bony ankles of the girl across from him. It's early in the summer, and no one has a real tan yet. But this girl's skin is white as paper. Like a bone, Sam thinks, looking at the naturally olive skin on the back of his hand. Her pallor makes the jutting angle of her ankle joint even sharper, above the black canvas of her faded sneakers and the gray of her flopping socks. The clangor of Angus' snail hitting the barrow, and Angus' murmuring laugh, startle Sam out of his minute examination. He stands up abruptly, confused.

"I seen you looking at that girl, Sam," Angus whispers. The ferry siren sounds again as the leading boat rounds the point and passes out of the bay and into the sound. Sam and Angus turn to watch the ferry disappear over the horizon. They remember a drawbridge they saw raised for a barge when they drove with Sam's dad to see their other grandparents, who live inland. Why isn't there a drawbridge there at the mouth of the bay? They imagine how huge it would be, raising and closing.

"Boys! Boys!" their boring Aunt Jean calls from the station door "Come in and eat your sandwiches!" She steps back inside.

Angus and Sam look at each other and groan. They scuff the sides of their shoes against the sun soft tar of the platform and look regretfully at the large head of snails collected in their wheelbarrow.

"Do we hafta?" Sam calls back finally. Angus crosses his arms across his chest and nods, although now there's no-one from their family at the station door- only some skinny old man in a brown suit looking irritable at his watch and clearing his throat. For a while no one answers, then,

"Sam! Angus!" their grandmother's voice cracks like a whip, brooking no argument. Sam looks furtively under his eyelashes across the track, to see if the skinny ankled girl is watching his humiliation. She's kneeling on the edge of the platform with a younger boy- he must be her brother- trying to pick an empty can up off the side of the tracks with a long stick that has been stripped of it's bark- she looks up at the noise of the wheelbarrow being dragged, and smiles at Sam in an inscrutable way for just an instant before she hooks the can and flips it upwards triumphantly onto her platform. The little boy claps and laughs.

"Sam!" Angus calls from the red brick station house, and Sam realizes he's been standing still. Blushing, he grabs the barrow handles and rushes to catch up to his cousin with his back to the paper pale girl.

"Don't you bring that dirty barrow in here, boys!" admonishes Aunt Jean, just as Angus starts to bump it down the short flight of steps. The boys complain, then settle for leaving it where they can watch it from inside.

From journal 85, a book mostly of drawings

TELL ME A RIDDLE & ANSWER ME TRUE-
WHAT IS THE CORE OF A KANGAROO?
ANSWER ME QUICKLY & ANSWER ME NOW-
WHICH WAY TO THE ID OF A COW?
THERE'S SO MANY THINGS THAT I NEVER WILL KNOW
AND SO MANY PLACES I NEVER WILL GO
SO PLEASE FEED THE HEART OF MY FRAGILE BELIEF-
NOW WHAT IS THE TRUTH TO A LEAF?

A SNAKE AS IT SLITHERS ITS WAY THROUGH THE GRASS
IS THINKING PERHAPS OF AN AEROPLANE CRASH-
THE SPIDER THAT SPINS HER STRONG WEB ROM A ROSE
IS PREENING AND STRIKING A SELF CONSCIOUS POSE-

SO TELL ME A RIDDLE AND ANSWER ME THIS
HOW DO TOADS DISCOVER BLISS?
ANSWER WITH HONESTY, COURAGE & SPEED-
WHAT DO DOGS REALLY NEED?
THINGS FALL TOGETHER IN MANY STRANGE WAYS
I'LL PUZZLE IT OUT TILL THE END OF MY DAYS
SO BE GENTLE, FRIEND, AND PLEASE TELL ME THE TRUTH-
WHY DON'T WE LIVE ON THE ROOF?

A BULL AS HE PRANCES ON SMALL DAINTY HOOVES
IS WINNING A CHESS GAME WITH ELEGANT MOVES;
A HORSE ON THE RUN WITH GREEN GRASS IN HER MOUTH
IS MAKING A MAP OF THE POST-BELLUM SOUTH

ONE LAST TIME I'LL BEG YOU TO SWIFLY EXPLAIN
WHY DOES A RABBIT GET WET IN THE RAIN?
TELL ME AS FAST AS EVER YOU CAN
WHY ISN'T A MONKEY A MAN?
EVERYTHING SEEMS TO JUST HAPPEN BY CHANCE
THIS LIFE IS AN INTRICATE SWIFT-MOVING DANCE
AND SO I ENTREAT YOU TO PLEASE HELP ME LEARN
WHY DOESN'T AN ICE-CUBE BURN?

From Journal 82, Sophia's last journal

Sailing to Byzantium

That is no country for old men. The young
In one another's arms, birds in the trees
-Those dying generations- at their song,
The salmon-falls, the mackerel-crowded seas,
Fish, flesh, or fowl, commend all summer long
Whatever is begotten, born and dies
Caught in that sensual music, all neglect
Monuments of unageing intellect.

An aged man is but a paltry thing,
A tattered coat upon a stick, unless
Soul clap it's hands and sing, and louder sing
For every tatter in its mortal dress,
Nor is there singing school but studying
Monuments of its own magnificence;
And therefore have I sailed the seas and come
To the holy city of Byzantium.

O sages standing in God's holy fire
As in the gold mosaic of a wall,
Come from the holy fire, perne in a gyre,
And be the singing-masters of my soul.
Consume my heart away; sick with desire
And fastened to a dying animal
It knows not what it is; and gather me
Into the artifice of eternity

Once out of nature I shall never take
My bodily shape from any natural thing
But such a form as Grecian goldsmiths make
Of hammered gold and gold enamelling
To keep a drowsy Emperor awake;
Or set upon a golden bough to sing
To lords and ladies of Byzantium
Of what is past, or passing, or to come.

Soul clap its hands and sing and louder sing
for every tatter in its mortal dress

We're headed for a head-on on the highway of love
coz you had my baby in your back seat
I'll blind you with my brights as I switch to four wheel drive
And I'll compact your compact up a treat

You made her pull a U-turn on the pathway of DESIRE
Now I'll have to drive you off the road
I'll be sitting pretty on my whitewall tires
Laughing while the county has you towed

I know that I shall meet my fate
somewhere among the clouds about;
Those that I fight I do not hate,
Those that I guard I do not love;
My country is Kiltartan Cross
my countrymen Kiltartan's poor
No likely end could bring them loss
Or leave them happier than before-
No law, nor duty bade me fight
Nor public men, nor cheering crowds,
A lonely impulse of delight
Lead to this tumult in the clouds;
I balanced all, brought all to mind
The years to come seemed waste of breath,
A waste of breath the years behind
In balance with this life, this death.

Unflinching Account of a Voyage in the Direction of HOPE & VIGOR

The rhyme of the temporaily confused hiker

in the soft mist she wandered through the wood
where white wet clouds were twined throughout the twigs
and damp dew in the droplets on mossy branches stood
while bright birds sang, perching on budded sprigs
there she did walk alone and nearly blind
for clouds that pressed their cloth against her eyes
stumbling in groves where random paths did wind
wandering down slopes and up the grassy rise
she felt uncertain ways with arms out-stretched
not knowing where she went she still pressed on
until the sun did rise and gold dawn sketched
bright bursts of light where she had tarried long
and drew back the dark covers of the mist
so that at last she stood and saw all 'round
where the brown branches from the trees did twist
and fresh sweet flowers rose forth from the ground
then in her heart relief burst like a song
she opened wide her arms and laughed out loud
til the does stopped and watched her with their young
the timid rabbit and the owl so proud,
the fox, the woodcock, starling and the bear
and every kind of beast throughout the wood
stopped at her laughter and in silence stared
struck by the sudden shifting of her mood
she laughed quite long and then made reckoning
by how the sun rose high of where she was
wise with good woodlore, craft and much cunning
she fed on honey while the bees did buzz
taking the dripping comb from out the tree
she drank sweet water from a sparkling rill
berries she found spread very plentifully
and of good food she soon had eat her fill
and so renewed by fruits and by beauty
since with the dark her terror had fast flown
she revelled in the greenswood's rich bounty

the mossy trunks of trees, and lichened stone,
the crystal streamlets coursing in their beds
fish leaping high and prey-birds stooping low
stags with their bony antlers so widespread
the grace of growth where'er her eyes did go
so full of joy she soon sang sweet and high
filling the air with anthems of her thanks
and half in dreams she walked with happy sighs
down the wide stream bed's green and vivid banks
til after time she came up to a place
where the tall trees gave way to meadowed ground
there at the forest's edge she turned to face
the highway home that her long search had found
and blessed to be on her way back to her home
still she stood moveless for a moment long
rich with remembering how she had restless roamed
and filled her heart with the wild forest's song-

O filthy sorrows of the soul
I am not free I am not whole
Abate, abate, begone, let go
& do not beat me to & fro
Disgusting vile and billious fear
go on, fuck off, get out of here
And as for you, o loathesome angst
I sicken of your tiresome pranks
PISS OFF AVAUNT & DISSIPATE
you children of horrific hate
What for? Because I so demand
to make myself at my command
a strong, autonomous, happy dyke
as free and happy AS I LIKE.

so mote it be

dated 2/16/93

"The Long ballad of common-sense"

Oh she's wrapped up in her downy bed
With pillows three beneath her head
But outside as the rain does fall
So does the wind's soft whisper call:

Come Luna heed my misty song
Where I with seagulls dance along
Oh enclos'd maiden trust this plea
Be wild and wanton- come with me

Oh wind and likewise falling rain
I fear the pow'r of your refrain
I must not stir from my warm home
Forever in the hills to roam

Oh Luna fear not all is well
With me the ferns and palm leaves tell-
Come count the blossoms and the vines
and step among the clustering pines

Oh wind it's true your voice is sweet
I feel an answer in me feet
But I have flesh as well as soul
and need a home to keep me whole

So long they riddle to and fro
Whether she shall stay or go
and Luna full of yearning fear
is half drawn by the rain's mild tear;

Oh sister wind but let me speak
and I this woman's heart will break-
Do you not hear the liquid thrill
that courses through each new-fed rill?

Do not you hear how sweet the sound
my wild tears make when hit the ground?
Luna come water o'er the earth
and nourish every plants rebirth-

Oh wind, oh rain, torment me not
with all the powers you have got
remember mercifully my bones
my heart my blood that are not stones

to stand outside of time and bear
unhous'd the season of the year
were I eternal I'd away
and tempest 'cross resistless days

How may I live through the cold
the storms, the clouds, the lightning bold
and how if I wondered through the sky
could earthborne woman learn to fly?

she pulls the quilt up to her ears
but still the urgent song she hears
the windows rattle and do shake
for elemental pleading's sake-

Bold Luna that do dare deny
the weeping rain, the wind's harsh cry
Know that we crave your warm blood's heat
Likewise the pulse of your heart's beat

Oh wind know that I crave thee too
For pow'r, for ceaseless moving through,
For thy eternal world wide might
But I must bide at home tonight

And rain! I love thee just as well
You fall upon the wave's high swell
You feed the streams and fill the brooks
and feed shy flowers in their nooks

You both I envy but cannot
Put off my short-lived human lot
Alas you doughty pow'rs will run
Long after my small time is done

She's wrapped up in her downy bed
with pillows three beneath her head
She's made her choice and will not roam
But still regrets the wind's dark moan

Within her dreams she hears the voice
Rejected by her cautious choice
And constantly within her ears
Echo the rain's resounding tears

Oh Luna come! Thou mortal shy
Put off your flesh, and time deny
Come, Luna, come, the wind still cries,
Share with my shout the cloudstrewn skies

Oh wind, oh rain, though my heart break
I may no other life-choice make
I am a child of season brief
A quick-used breath, a falling leaf

And so I bid you sad farewell
No matter what mad joys you tell
I will not step outside my hearth
To dance above the storm swept earth

On The Infinite Distraction of Abstract Thought

"What is Never?" quoth the Bard
wrestling with the Léopard
of Abstract Thought, all entwined
In Formless Snares cast by the Mind

"What, if it may come to that
Is Always?" she demanded then
speaking straight into her Hat
and through it, and then out again.

Nothing receiving as reply
Dauntèd the Poet makes to sigh
But here is thwarted too, because
She's quick distracted by the Buzz

Of leaping Concepts, quick Ideas
That vault across her echo'd Skull-
See, she pursues them- Reader, see her
Limping, hopeless chase the Gull

Swift wingèd of Elusive Thought
Attractive, Brilliant, still Uncaught
Where, weaving arcs of Wisdom Bright
Within the Mists of Mental Night

It darts, o Thrilling Bird, across
Great Heavens of Philosophy
She glimpses it but then 'tis lost
Cached in the Cloud's Unclarity
Poor Poet She must ever Pace
Through Labrynths hid behind her Face.

GIVE UP RELAX, YOU DONT HAVE TO!

Never Never
Never Never
Never Never Know
Why it is and
How it is and
Where it is you go

Ever Ever
Ever Ever
Ever Ever Ask
What it is and
If this is and
If there *is* a Task

Wonder, Ponder
Wander, Founder
Blunder Hunting for
Where it is and
If it is and
Who it is you are-

Questing, Testing
Never Resting
Stressing to define
Forever all the
Fluid Fluxes
Of Th'Infinite Mind-
Try to Climb a Mountain Backwards in the Dark of Night
Upside down Against the Wind-
well, I S'pose you *Might*...

Sir Miriam McPiffle de Drivelwoode, 1710.

Foolishly Frantic

Foolishly Frantic she Forever Felt
Desperate Desires to Delve Deep in the Dark
Of Ever-Increasing, Endless, Infinite Thought-
that Ceaseless Expanding Sea wherein no Spark
Stemming to Search out from a Single Soul
Alone can carry all the concatenations
Of Reason- Random and Resistless Roils
Grow in Unguessed-at Glorious Aggregation
Too Mighty for one Mind, too Manifold
Too Myriad, too Many and Too Much
She who would Solve this, stubbornly resolved
Still Saw she must Surrender before Such-
Thus with a Sorrowing Shriek she Somersaulted
Home a humbler heart and, hopeless, halted-

Am I here
O indeed I suppose I am
and what other evidence is there
really beyond that?
No other proof but this:
I think it so
At any rate it cannot be disproved
that I am here
Always in evidence is my
interpretation, endless
no matter of what
the smallest information serves to show
my thought
(conscious or otherwise)
is ceaseless- and
as long as I interpret something
(right or wrong) there's
something to interpret
its essential verity outside my mind
being thus shown to be
rather beside the point (to me)
AMEN

cling earth and wrap me warm

cling earth and wrap me warm
all in sensation sense and sensuality
all-flowered senses BLOOM and seize
each feeling at its fullest – Aye, allow
touch to be final, the last lasting prooof
of self, of simple joy, even ecstasy -
Presence here among all living things
and my connection with them through my life
grant me that easy peace-
HUMM little bees among the stamens HUMM
Custy with pollen bright with airborne LIFE
Hop frogs in the rivers CLIMB AMONG THE TREES
remind me, flowers hanging on your vines
bright colored bursts of brilliant evergy
laden with ants, with aphids, with all BUGS
REMIND me endless entwining CHAIN OF LIFE
that EVEN HERE wrapped in the cold gray city sky
I still am RAPT with AWE with JOY with PEACE
and POWERLESSNESS before the ETERNITY and
CHANGELESS CHANGE of FLUIDFLEXING ever
REFRESHED LIFE!!! YES YES YES YES-

“The Rant Pentameter”

the little doubts and sorrows of my mind
are gray as mist and as impermanent
remember SOPHY tiny happy child
intelligent with hope, with energy
LAUGHING SMALL BABY clutching with fat hands
at nothing and regretting nothing long
That's the essential self, the delighted eye
learning anew each day the awe of all
it sees, excited and inspired to reach out for
what I may or again may not some time receive
HEY little serious child staring at worms
isn't it MARVELLOUS how they work their way
slowly forever through the heavy soil
lifting and changing everything they pass
how gray, disgusting, wet, how wonderful,
how strange, how simple, complex, without end,
how always, how sufficient to itself,
how real to touch and every other sense
MMM! Let me eat it, or let it eat me
(at a later date, not yet to be arranged)
NOW with this STUNNED ECSTATIC THRILL
which is a religious vision in some way
Particular and powerful, grace ephemeral-
How may I humbly ask does it apply
to RENT? or WAGES? LAUNDRY? GROCERIES?
What, once I see the butterfly
landing for instants on the flower's edge
do I do with this delight, which doesn't seem
really to recognize too much beyond itself,
having no taste for traffic or for clouds
of toxic gas released by greedy fools?-
It is regenerative it does restore
BUT IT DON'T PAY MY BILLS AND NOR DO I-
so, if a humble human may enquire
(as transient to time as any ant,
impermanent caterpillar or fading star)
What should I do next? How will I know?
and, if it's not too much- saving your grace
COULD I BE HAPPY?

COLLD IT BE ARRANGED that this
Entrancèd Eye
might serve its servant on some
PRACTICAL PLANE???

Sir Jane Playne de Graye 1530

HOMILY: ON NEVER KNOWING

HAPPY THE HEART WHICH IS UNCERTAIN
ALL WAYS EXERTED TOWARDS DELIGHT
THRILLINGLY SPYING ON THE CURTAIN
OF THE FUTURE- WHAT IT MIGHT
OR MIGHT NOT YET REVEAL TO EYES
YEARNING FOR SIGNS OF WHAT'S TO COME
SEE! TH'ANTICIPATORY SIGNS
STRAIGHT OUTWEIGH THE VAST HUMDRUM
OF CLAIMING TO BE SURE ALREADY
OF WHAT AWAITS US IN THE NEXT
PREDESTINED SCENE- YEA! HOW PETTY
'TIS TO HAVE BY ONE THE TEXT
READ THROUGH BEFORE HAND OF THE DRAMA
BETTER SURE T'EXPELT BUT THIS:
WHETHER IT'S COMIC, BLAND, OR TRAUMA
IN THE UNKNOWING IS THE BLISS!

THUS, GOOD MY FRIEND AND PATIENT READER
MAKE I MY CASE WITH NO PRETENSE:-
LIFE, AS YE SEE IT, IS A THEATER-
MY! BUT THE STAGE IS QUITE IMMENSE!

SIR EMILY VANDERBILGE VON CUCKOOSDORF

from journal 59
dated 9.20.96

Your kitchen table

Your kitchen table is under the window-
yellow light on plums and apples- and
sometimes we sat there; the air
carved our bodies out of space,
our movements were contiguous and occasionally
overlapping and I anxiously made breakfast
while you wished I were more powerful-

You wanted to be patient- your tenderness,
oblique and inferential,
carved space between our bodies- rarely touching-
You thought I was a bag of apples brought
up from a bin in the cellar,
crisp sometimes, and sometimes
winy, mealy, soft and heavy- or sometimes
sweet, refreshing- Your tongue
curled back in your mouth, hoping I'd please you,
knowing you couldn't rely on me-

What should be happening?
Separate is how we started, it's how we've
ended up for now-
I thought you were a house I wanted to live in-
never could find the door- instead I
climbed down chimneys, squeezed through windows,
every entrance but the most direct-
looking for welcome I wandered in you,
waiting for the alarm to go off-

You wished I were more powerful; I wished
you were more tender- I
pointed my mind at you like a camera,
tried to take pictures of what I thought
should be happening-
waiting for the alarm to go off, I wandered in you-
light fell on the walls of empty rooms in
tilted bars- I sat down at your piano
and played a chain of hesitating chords-
in the next room, listening, you heard
my tentative music; you tried to be,
you wanted to be patient-

Your kitchen table is under the window-
yellow light on plums and apples-
the air is full of tenderness and power
colliding in the space between us-

From the folder entitled "First Versions"

I saw you here

I saw you here today again
after another winter gone, a year now
since we met, almost a year since-
things were said, and now you're
back again, a little visit,
because times change.

the winter's back and so are you,
milder this time. Soon we'll be able
to look each other in the eyes
and maybe trust. Round in the
season's inevitable circle we're taken
learning and learning again

to see the same things, differently.
New eyes, new details. Maybe each spring
the shoot uncurls and hurts
the unsuspecting soil with growth, maybe it's
one of those difficult bargains:
what you give for what you get. Another risk.

Things are still hard to say, still awkward-
we still stand uncertain face to face
but it's winter again; times change with
or without us it would seem- circumstances alter,
build new facts   Maybe this time
this visit we can uncurl a little

spread our leaves a little like that ivy plant
you came to pick up for a friend.   The reason
for your visit, not just to come.   We still
need reasons to see each other's face
to be expected- pain don't slip off like it should:
old husk, new rose- but growing's slow.

rangoon

rangoon
I have never been to rangoon
but I am told oh exotic fantasy
they have elephants   in that area

elephants are ok I guess
I would like maybe someday to ride in a howdah
("howdah?"   " Oh, I'm fine – and you?")

never no never
with bright yeller malarial dysfunction
will I trample
the weedy warped and verdant jungles
of afrik nor yet
india my dear

nor jaundice
though perhaps I'll snare in blandness
the singing winging
weave-and-winding slurp and burp
twerpitude of 24hr flu
oh sons of mine
oh fever-ridden daughters

who knows if it troubles me that I
must drift? I'm
swaddled simply in the time
alotted; I drift, and in time who knows mayhap shall see
rangoon
rangoon rangoon rangoon

Sight fractured

Lips like sudden dragonflies
tasting surprised the flooded honey
down my throat – become
astonished;
I pass like blindness flashes of
you back, your hands...

Voiceless my shivering. I live
here on the edge of thigh,
your evening light embracing me and
motion – of everything combined-
forever words disdains and time
darting like lizard's tongue-
your eyes and mine

might be lasting eternally. My eyes absorb
parts of you, broken in glass moonlight. Dark
lies here, exhausted.

the moon is a madwoman

the moon is a madwoman
who likes cats she
stalks the sky drinking
gin from a silver hipflask and
spitting tobacco juice into black holes
the moon is a bulldyke
I shall want. She leadeth me through
dark partures and
lights her match on the heel of her
combat boot-

She has a face like Jimmy Dean
gone old and drunk
She's sort of beautiful the way
she walks so proud.
Under her arm she carries a gun
as she walks through the fields,
and pots her a rabbit for dinner,
damning the vermin.

The moon is a hermit I
love her
And every night I climb a ladder to kiss her but
she don't come near
She built this house with her own
two hands before any of us were born
And now she can sit on her porch,
to watch it all pass on.

"Yes," she says; that's all she
ever wants to say.

The moon is a dagger she stabs me through
Lord I desire her, that tough old flesh.
She's got plenty of tasks to
attend to, yes, I know-
Running a place on your own you
can never sit down it seems sometimes-

The moon is no shirker, better believe
some night
I wake to find her gone;
she leaves a note
"Back soon sweetheart gone for a walk,
back soon"
But it's hard to know if she will be-
she's her own
and nobody knows it better. One hard moon.

As I went wandering

As I went wandering in the desert
    (I never went wandering in the desert)
I bent to pick up a small gray stone
    (in projections or dreams)
And the sky was blankly blue above me
    (or so I imagine it might be
            in the heat)

Oh I wished I could get a drink of clear water
such as I often had in the days before this dream
when I was one of those tall women sitting in a
red chair at a desk, thinking political thoughts and
raking together my achievements
in the name
of a viable future

And my heart beat hard, standing there in all the miles of sand
thinking there should be at least one bird
slicing a dark curve out of all that long clear sky
remembering the notes I used to make in the margins of
memoranda while I looked down out the window
at the foreshortened people
who walked directly from one place to another

Out there in the desert my mind burst like a
bomb
there was a cinderdust in the air and I felt sure
that as I walked bones slid
grainily under the sand. No birds in the air and
my hands empty.

I am thinking about the end of the world
when there will be nothing at all to look at.

Listen honey I

Listen honey I
am a tree and you
are the place I sink my
roots – you say

it hurts but trees
don't hear the soil
complaining:

let me drink you up,
I'll fill
my veins with you and swell

burstingly full, my branches
wrapped
around your limbs, my leaves
budding into your bones -

you think I'm cruel but
honey I'm just here

You have to know

I.

You have to know where your dreams come from;
the night, singing lately
sorrowful songs, that
melt attention blind; you

don't know where you're headed and it's all
TOO LOUD, you're
standing in some supermarket
looking for a can of Instant ME,
under these bright stark striplights baby
mumbling out
your koans of identitiy-
(its always the BRAND NEW INSTANT, here,
with added *oomph*)

II.

Where we come from lover nothing
has a centre to it.
or the story of:

Up on E. 78th the gray old men
look into bakeries, they
lean out 2nd story windows,
slouch on their fire-escapes,
talk about the rent, falsetto
age in stubbled chins- it's
what is called "a succession of images", love
-you always seem to think
you notice where you put yourself-

dogs piss on the hydrants.
And which image
do you want to make important now?
Today we praise our lovers' hands:
It's a tradition,
honey, it's
Romance:

" HONEY I NEVER LOVED ANYONE
(LIKE I LOVE YOU)"

III.

Listen you have eyes like photographs
of the usual day: People
have different ways
of categorizing,
darling; "It's always a bumpy ride"
they say- which platitude
most satisfies? And do you know
how to hold yourself? It's
all a question of attitude.

IV.

OH, you can't ever know where
you aren't or where
you really won't be soon
(though the sense of touch is a
general guide to where you might be)
Which part of Big Truth do
you include, in your daily sermon
('Member, hafta talk in the vernacular or you'll never
MAKE IT TO THE BIG TIME)

Leaves me wondering-
how many secret selves could be there
dancing out there in the shadow-dark?
What You Didn't Tell Daddy
What You Hid From The Lord...

Dismember a memory sweetie as
Time Crawls By
                    you got your
mean joe jive indifferent death plays
disco in the lounge
for some strung out maiden
from some standby town where
dusk to dawn the
trucks drag through a

racket of engines and beer,
and all the boys are
shouting corporate come, like a
golden shower: they got to
glorify their tristesse urine

"In case of approaching senility
please make Eden out of your ass
twat clit cunt tits of
throbbing member"   (Lean-over-honey-an
spreadem, who knows
you might be next
to give up in some
          cinematic alleyway)

GET YOUR NICE HOT
picture of every instant
ever employed PLUS*BONUS*PLUS
one complete synthesis, disgusting
in its respect for detail.

I-2-3 and
everybody grabs a
version of themselves from the discount warehouse
(So where would I have been just then
if I hadn't been
Kissing You
when you sat there
on the white rock, like the
nymph on the soda logo? Well you know- love
is a permanent matter of infinite series-)

V.

"Life," she said "is not contained
            by any perception of it that I
            can produce, not even snagged
            for an instant on the intersti
             ces of my cosmographical sur-
           vey I
           got here",
                                she said, "so

turn the radio on let's drink
some beer
slouched down by the
leatherette 'n' vinyl
kitchen table-
because
that's what one does
on slimy sleazy
deeply queasy
Sunday afternoons" she said,
and "stirred by beauty we are sometimes
stirred by beauty- oh, but
not right now", she said.

this handwritten poem was water-stained and parts of it are illegible

Dreamed I jumped in a love-taxi

Dreamed I jumped in a love-taxi
drove around, checked out
the scene. There it was:
dirty dusty city.

Dreamed love rented her
          apartment to me.
spending time cleaning up,
washing desire and passion
off the walls
scrubbing love-mold off
the shower stalls,
Love-grease
off the kitchen ceiling.
Called in the exterminator-
roaches got too bad.

Dreamed I went down to the river and
stepped in the shore of romance
bit me in my face
and shook me, shook me, danced me
down-
blub, blub,
down there in those darksome waves

Dreamed I heard the love bird sing
            -jungles, she
ear   trumpet
flew
up in those sunlit leaves

Love-cat pounced, she
           rolled me
kissed me hard
all purrs
and claws she
arched

and hissed
silked up around my ankles, sighing

Love-snake
        shared her apple
she said
        "Look," I looked.
Love snake coiled and danced
all green and slick, slip, slid away

When I wake up late,
there are apple seeds under my pillow.
Apple seeds stuck all over my
skin, and floating in my
coffee. Love misting up the mirror
while I brush my teeth,
there it is. Leaking out of the walls.